How to Get Rich Doing Business in Mexico

Mexico Business Guide and Contacts

I0483141

By

Patrick W. Nee

The Internationalist
www.internationalist.com

<u>Other Titles Featured in the Business Guides Series</u>

MAKING MONEY IN CHINA: Key Business
Contacts and Addresses

MAKING MONEY IN CHINA: China Business
Guide and Contacts

MAKING MONEY IN CHINA: China Country
Guide for Businesses

MAKING MONEY IN RUSSIA: Russia Country
Guide for Businesses

MAKING MONEY IN EXPORTING: A
Complete Guide to the Business of Exporting

MAKING MONEY IN BRAZIL: Brazil Business
Guide and Contacts

The Internationalist®

International Business, Investment, and Travel

Published by:
The Internationalist Publishing Company
96 Walter Street/Suite 200
Boston MA 02131, USA
Tel: 617-354-7722
www.internationalist.com
PN@internationalist.com

Copyright © 2014 by PWN

Welcome to the **Internationalist Business Guides** series:

The key to a successful business is knowing the markets. HOW TO GET RICH DOING BUSINESS IN MEXICO: MEXICO BUSINESS GUIDE AND CONTACTS offers executives, investors, and entrepreneurs the need-to-know information about doing business in Mexico.

Written as an in-depth, straightforward reference guide, this book lists key information about the Turkish market, its challenges, and opportunities. It then looks into a dozen of Turkey's leading industries, their backgrounds, current situation, and projected course.

Whether you are looking to break into international business or need to update your knowledge on Turkish markets— this comprehensive guide is for you.

The Internationalist

Contents

Chapter 1:Doing Business in Mexico

  Market Overview

  Market Challenges

  Market Opportunities

  Market Entry Strategy

Chapter 2: Political and Economic Environment

  U.S.-Mexico Relations

  U.S. Security Cooperation with Mexico

  Bilateral Economic Relations

  Mexico's Membership in International Organizations

  Bilateral Representation

Chapter 3:Selling U.S. Products and Services

  Using an Agent or Distributor

  Establishing an Office

  Franchising

  Direct Marketing

  Joint Ventures/Licensing

  Selling to the Government

  Distribution and Sales Channels

  Selling Factors/Techniques

  Electronic Commerce

  Trade Promotion and Advertising

  Pricing

  Sales Service/Customer Support

  Protecting Your Intellectual Property

  Due Diligence

  Local Professional Services

Chapter 4: Leading Sectors for U.S. Export and Investment

Agribusiness

Automotive Parts and Supplies

Education and Training Services

Energy Sector

(Traditional)

Environmental Sector

Franchising Sector

Housing and Construction

Internet and IT Services

IT Health Care

Medical Devices

Packaging Equipment

Plastic Materials/Resins

Renewable Energy

Security and Safety Equipment and Services

Smart Grid

Telecommunications Equipment

Transportation Infrastructure Equipment and Services

Travel and Tourism Services

Agricultural Sector

Chapter 5: Trade Regulations and Standards

Import Tariffs

Trade Barriers

Import Requirements and Documentation

U.S. Export Controls

Temporary Entry

Labeling and Marking Requirements

Prohibited and Restricted Imports

Customs Regulations and Contact Information

Standards

Trade Agreements

Web Resources

Chapter 6: Investment Climate

Openness to Foreign Investment

Conversion and Transfer Policies

Expropriation and Compensation

Dispute Settlement

Performance Requirements and Incentives

Right to Private Ownership and Establishment

Protection of Property Rights

Transparency of Regulatory System

Efficient Capital Markets and Portfolio Investment

Competition from State Owned Enterprises

Corporate Social Responsibility

Political Violence

Corruption

Bilateral Investment Agreements

OPIC and Other Investment Insurance Programs

Labor

Foreign Trade Zones/Free Ports

Foreign Direct Investment Statistics

Web Resources

Chapter 7: Trade and Project Financing

How Do I Get Paid (Methods of Payment)

How Does the Banking System Operate

Foreign-Exchange Controls

U.S. Banks and Local Correspondent Banks

Project Financing

Web Resources

Chapter 8: Business Travel

Business Customs

Travel Advisory

Visa Requirements

Telecommunications

Transportation

Language

Health

Local Time, Business Hours and Holidays

Temporary Entry of Materials and Personal Belongings

Web Resources

Chapter 9: Contacts, Market Research, and Trade Events

Contacts

Market Research

Trade Events

Chapter 10: Guide to Our Services

Chapter 1: Doing Business in Mexico

Market Overview

The North American Free Trade Agreement (NAFTA), which was enacted in 1994 and created a free trade zone for Mexico, Canada, and the United States,is the most important feature in the U.S.-Mexico bilateral commercial relationship.

Mexico is the United States' 3rd largest trade partner and 2nd largest export market for U.S. products.

U.S-Mexico bilateral trade increased from $88 billion in 1993, the year prior to the implementation of NAFTA, to $460 billion in 2011, an increase of 423 percent.

Mexico is the most populated Spanish speaking country in the world and has 112 million people with 78% living in urban areas. 10% of the population is considered wealthy class and about 45% in poverty earning less than USD $10 per day. The remaining 45% of the population is considered middle class. Mexico has a very young population with a median age of 27. It offers a large market with a GDP of approximately USD $1.1 trillion. Per capita income is USD $15,100.

With a shared Western and Hispanic culture U.S. producers find it easier to market and sell their services and products in Mexico.

There is a large installed base of manufacturing in a wide range of sectors.

Mexico is a stable democracy.

Mexico has bounced back strongly from 2009's worldwide recession. In 2011
Mexico-United States bilateral trade increased by 17 percent from 2010 levels and Mexico's GDP increased by 3.9 percent.

Market Challenges

Mexico's size and diversity are often under appreciated by U.S. exporters. It can be difficult to find a single distributor or agent to cover this vast market.

The Mexican legal system differs in many significant ways from the U.S. system. U.S. firms should consult with competent legal counsel before entering into any business agreements with Mexican partners.

The banking system in Mexico has shown signs of growth after years of stagnation, but interest rates remain relatively high. In particular, small and medium-sized enterprises (SMEs) find it difficult to obtain financing at reasonable rates despite Mexican Government efforts to increase capital for SMEs. U.S. companies need to conduct thorough due diligence before entering into business with a Mexican firm, and should be conservative in extending credit and alert to payment delays. As one element in a prudent due diligence process, the U.SCommercial Service offices in Mexico can conduct background checks on potential Mexican partners. U.S. companies should assist Mexican buyers explore financing options, including Export-Import Bank programs.

Mexican customs regulations, product standards and labor laws may present pitfalls for U.S. companies. U.S. Embassy commercial, agricultural and labor attachés are available to counsel firms with respect to regulations that affect their particular export product or business interest.

Mexico will elect a new President on July 1, 2012. Sales to the Mexican federal government will likely slow down in mid 2012 as the new President develops his Administration.

Violence among transnational criminal organizations has created insecurity in parts of Mexico, particularly in some border areas. Prior to traveling to Mexico it is strongly recommended to review the Department of State's travel guidance related to Mexico.

Market Opportunities

Abundant market opportunities for U.S. firms exist in Mexico; trade totals more than $1 billion a day between the two countries.

Mexico's geographic proximity to the United States has propelled the maquiladora industry near the U.S.-Mexico border and currently gives U.S. businesses an alternative to Asia-based manufacturing and opportunities to sell into the supply chain.

Some of Mexico's most promising sectors include: agribusiness; auto parts & services; education services; energy; environmental; franchising; housing & construction; packaging equipment; plastics and resins; security & safety equipment and services; technology sectors; transportation infrastructure equipment and services; travel & tourism services and the agricultural sector.

A complete list of the top prospects in Mexico is provided in Chapter Four. However, given the size of the Mexican market, there are numerous other promising prospects, including food processing equipment, architectural and engineering services and more. If an industry is not explicitly mentioned as a "best prospect," it does not necessarily mean that there are not ample opportunities in the Mexican market.

Market Entry Strategy

To do business in Mexico it is key to develop and maintain close relationships with clients and partners. Mexicans prefer direct communication such as telephone calls or face-to-face meetings. However, e-mail is widely used.

Mexican companies are extremely price conscious, seek financing options, tend to desire exclusive agreements, and value outstanding service and flexibility.

U.S. firms wishing to export to Mexico will find a variety of market entry strategies. Many factors help determine the best strategy, such as the product/service, logistics & customs, distribution, marketing, direct or indirect sales, exporting experience, and language proficiency, among others.

The U.S. Commercial Service can assess market potential of products and service, provide advice on export strategies, and facilitate business agreements

Chapter 2: Political and Economic Environment

U.S.-Mexico Relations

U.S. relations with Mexico are important and complex. The two countries share a 2,000-mile border, and bilateral relations between the two have a direct impact on the lives and livelihoods of millions of Americans, whether the issue is trade and economic reform, homeland security, drug control, migration, or the environment. The scope of U.S.-Mexican relations is broad and goes beyond diplomatic and official contacts, and entails extensive commercial, cultural, and educational ties, with over 1.25 billion dollars of two-way trade and roughly one million legal border crossings each day. In addition, a million American citizens live in Mexico. U.S. tourists to Mexico numbered over 20.3 million in 2012 making Mexico the top destination of U.S. travelers. Mexican tourists to the U.S. were about 13.4 million in 2011, and they spent some $9.2 billion.

Cooperation between the United States and Mexico along the common border includes state and local problem-solving mechanisms; transportation planning; and institutions to address resource, environment and health issues. In 2010, a high level Executive Steering Committee for 21st Century Border Management was created to spur advancements in creating a modern, secure, and efficient border. The multi-agency U.S.-Mexico Binational Group on Bridges and Border Crossings meets twice yearly to improve the efficiency of existing crossings and coordinate planning for new ones. The ten U.S. and Mexican border states are active participants in these meetings. Chaired by U.S. and Mexican consuls, Border Liaison Mechanisms operate in "sister city" pairs and have proven to be an effective means of dealing with a variety of local issues including border infrastructure, accidental violation of sovereignty by law enforcement officials, charges of mistreatment of foreign nationals, and cooperation in public health matters.

The United States and Mexico have a long history of cooperation on environmental and natural resource issues, particularly in the border area, where there are serious environmental problems caused by rapid population growth, urbanization, and industrialization. Cooperative activities between the U.S. and Mexico take place under a number of arrangements such as the U.S.-Mexico Border 2012/2020 Program; the North American Development Bank and the Border Environment Cooperation Commission; the North American Commission for Environmental Cooperation; the Border Health Commission; and a variety of other agreements that address border health, wildlife and migratory birds, national parks, forests, and marine and atmospheric resources. The International Boundary and Water Commission, created by a treaty between the United States and Mexico, is an international organization responsible for managing a wide variety of water resource and boundary preservation issues.

The two countries also have cooperated on telecommunications services in the border area for more than 50 years. Recent border agreements cover mobile broadband services, including smartphones, and similar devices. The High Level Consultative Commission on Telecommunications continues to serve as the primary bilateral arena for both governments to promote growth in the sector and to ensure compatible services in the border area. The United States and Mexico are implementing an agreement to improve cross-border public security communications in the border area.

In May 2013, the formation of a Bilateral Forum on Higher Education, Innovation, and Research was announced. Through this forum, the U.S. and Mexican governments will encourage broader access to quality post-secondary education for traditionally underserved demographic groups, especially in the science, technology, engineering, and mathematics (STEM) fields. They will also seek to expand educational exchanges, promote joint research in areas of mutual interest, and share best practices in higher education and innovation. This work builds upon the many productive educational and research linkages between U.S. and Mexican academic institutions, civil society, and the private sector.

U.S. Security Cooperation with Mexico

The Merida Initiative is an unprecedented partnership between the United States and Mexico to address violence and criminality while strengthening the rule of law and the respect for human rights. Since 2010, our Merida Initiative cooperation has been organized under four strategic pillars. The first pillar aims to disrupt the capacity of organized crime to operate and the second pillar focuses on enhancing the capacity of Mexico's government and institutions to sustain the rule of law. The Merida Initiative's third pillar aims to improve border management to facilitate legitimate trade and movement of people while thwarting the flow of drugs, arms, and cash. Finally, the fourth pillar seeks to build strong and resilient communities.

U.S. cooperation with Mexico under the Merida Initiative directly supports programs to help Mexico train its police forces in modern investigative techniques, promote a culture of lawfulness, and implement key justice reforms. Through fiscal year 2012, the U.S. Congress has appropriated $1.9 billion for the Merida Initiative. U.S. Agency for International Development (USAID) programs under the Merida Initiative support Mexican efforts to address key challenges to improving citizen security and well-being, developing and testing models to mitigate the community-level impact of crime and violence, and support Mexico's implementation of criminal justice constitutional reforms that protect citizens' rights. Additional USAID programs support Mexico's commitment to reducing greenhouse gas emissions and to enhancing economic competitiveness to improve citizens' lives.

Bilateral Economic Relations

The U.S. and Mexico, along with Canada, are partners in the North American Free Trade Agreement (NAFTA) and enjoy a broad and expanding trade relationship. Through the North American Leaders' Summits, the United States, Canada, and Mexico cooperate to improve North American competitiveness, ensure the safety of their citizens, and promote clean energy and a healthy environment. The three nations also cooperate on hemispheric and global challenges, such as managing transborder infectious diseases and seeking greater integration to respond to challenges of transnational organized crime.

Mexico is the United States' second-largest export market (after Canada) and third-largest trading partner (after Canada and China). In 2012, two-way merchandise trade reached nearly $500 billion. Mexico's exports rely heavily on supplying the U.S. market, but the country has also sought to diversify its export destinations. Nearly 78 percent of Mexico's exports in 2012 went to the United States. In 2012, Mexico was the third-largest supplier of foreign crude oil to the United States, as well as the largest export market for U.S. refined petroleum products and a growing market for U.S. natural gas. Top U.S. exports to Mexico include electrical machinery, nuclear equipment, motor vehicle parts, mineral fuels and oils, and plastics.

U.S. companies have invested $101 billion in Mexico. Mexican investment in the United States has grown by over 11 percent in the past year to $27.9 billion.

Mexico is a major recipient of remittances, sent mostly from Mexicans in the United States, totaling over $22.4 billion in 2012. Most remittances are used for immediate consumption -- food, housing, health care, education -- but some collective remittances, sent from Mexican migrants in the U.S. to their community of origin, are used for shared projects and infrastructure improvements under Mexico's 3 for 1 program that matches contributions with federal, state and local funds.

In May 2013, the High Level Economic Dialogue (HLED) was established to further elevate and strengthen the U.S.-Mexico bilateral commercial and economic relationship. The HLED, which will be led at the cabinet level, is envisioned as a flexible platform intended to advance strategic economic and commercial priorities central to promoting mutual economic growth, job creation, and competitiveness. The HLED is expected to meet annually, starting fall of 2013, to facilitate dialogue and joint initiatives and to promote shared approaches to regional and global economic leadership. It will build on, but not duplicate, a range of existing successful bilateral dialogues and working groups.

Mexican investment in the United States has grown by over 35 percent the past five years. It is the seventh fastest growing investor country in the United States.

Mexico is making progress in its intellectual property rights enforcement efforts, although piracy and counterfeiting rates remain high. The United States placed Mexico on the Watch List in the 2013 Special 301 report. The U.S. continues to work with the Mexican Government to implement its commitment to improving intellectual property protection.

Mexico joined the Trans-Pacific Partnership (TPP) negotiations in 2012, which will establish new and higher standards for global trade. In 2012, Mexico joined Chile, Colombia, and Peru to launch an ambitious regional economic integration effort, the Alliance of the Pacific.

Mexico's Membership in International Organizations

Mexico is a strong supporter of the United Nations (UN) and Organization of American States (OAS) systems, and hosted the G-20 Leaders' Summit in 2012. Mexico and the United States belong to a number of the same international organizations, including the UN, OAS, Asia-Pacific Economic Cooperation (APEC) forum, G-20, Organization for Economic Cooperation and Development (OECD), International Monetary Fund (IMF), World Bank (WB), and World Trade Organization (WTO). In 2012, Mexico became a member of the Wassenaar Arrangement, a multilateral export control regime for conventional arms and dual-use goods. In 2013, Mexico joined the Australia Group, an informal forum of countries which, through the harmonization of export controls, seeks to ensure that exports do not contribute to the development of chemical or biological weapons.

Bilateral Representation

The U.S. Ambassador to Mexico is E. Anthony Wayne; other principal embassy officials are listed in the Department's Key Officers List.

Mexico maintains an embassy in the United States at 1911 Pennsylvania Ave. NW, Washington, DC 20006 (tel. 202-728-1600).

Chapter 3: Selling U.S. Products and Services

Using an Agent or Distributor

Many U.S. firms find it useful and/or necessary to use a distributor to distribute their products in Mexico. They can be used to distribute products in various regions and to a variety of businesses. Using a distributor is also efficient when products are required to be in stock and readily available.

Some U.S. firms sell their products through a sales agent. Usually, a sales agent is an individual. However, some Mexican firms are interested in serving as sales agents for U.S. firms. Sales agents can be effective in reaching smaller cities and remote locations in Mexico.

Selection of an appropriate agent or distributor requires time and effort. There may be many qualified candidates and U.S. firms should be careful and use high standards in order to select a qualified and appropriate agent/distributor.Since most Mexican firms sell in a limited area, U.S. companies should consider appointing representatives in multiple cities to broaden distribution. It is usually not advisable to grant an exclusive, national agreement. It is important to develop a close working relationship with the appointed agent/distributor. Providing appropriate training, marketing support, samples, product support, and timely supply of spare parts is critical for success. There are no indemnity laws to prevent a company from canceling an agent or distributor agreement, but the cancellation clause should be specific. Sales performance clauses in agent/distributor agreements are permitted, and failure to meet established standards can be a reasonable cause for contract cancellation.

Before signing an agent/distributor agreement, all parties should fully understand the terms and conditions and the relationship to be developed. Many relationships are strained because insufficient time is invested in developing a full understanding of what is expected.

The Commercial Service and other organizations, such as the American Chamber of Commerce in Mexico and U.S. state government representative offices, maintain lists of Mexican agents/distributors, manufacturers, Mexican government offices, and private sector trade organizations. After identifying a suitable agent/distributor, the U.S. exporter is strongly encouraged to conduct a commercial background check on the Mexican firm. The U.S. Commercial Service offers an International Company Profile report that provides background information on a potential business partner.

If the product is new to the market, or if the market is extremely competitive, advertising and other promotional support should be negotiated in detail with your representative. Product and industry knowledge, track record, enthusiasm, and commitment should be weighed heavily. It is suggested that the U.S. exporter schedule annual visits of Mexican personnel to the U.S. company for training. Another factor to consider is financing, as credit from Mexican banks is limited and when available has high interest rates. Joint venture arrangements should also be investigated to strengthen market penetration. Direct marketing and telemarketing are still evolving marketing strategies, but they are gaining in popularity and scope.

Establishing an Office

For U.S. companies interested in establishing a presence in Mexico, the General Law of Mercantile Organizations (or the Civil Code) regulates many different forms of business entities. The type of business incorporation that a U.S. company or individual chooses is extremely important, as it determines the operations they are allowed to perform in Mexico and, among other liabilities, the amount of taxes they pay.

Some of the most commonly used types of business classifications are the Sociedad Anonima (Corporation) identified with "S.A." at the end of the company name, and the Sociedad Anonima de Capital Variable (Corporation with Variable Capital) identified with "S.A. de C.V." One of the advantages of the latter is that the minimum fixed capital can be changed subsequent to the initial formation.

Limited Liability Partnership (Sociedad de Responsabilidad Limitada) identified with "S. de R.L." is similar to a closed corporation in the United States and has the option of having variable capital (S. de R.L. de C.V.). As this is an organization formed by individuals, it has similar characteristics to a partnership with the exception of unlimited liability.

Civil Partnership (Sociedad Civil) is the most common organization for professional service providers. It has no minimum capital requirement and no limit on the number of partners, but it is taxable in the same way as a corporation. It is identified with "S.C."

Civil Association (Asociación Civil) is the form that charitable or nonprofit organizations adopt to operate and is identified with "A.C." A foreign company may open a branch ("sucursal") in Mexico as an alternative to incorporating. A branch can provide rights and responsibilities similar to a corporation, including tax liability and access to local courts, but requires the approval of the National Foreign Investment Commission. It is recommended to consult with a law firm in Mexico prior to establishing an office here.

Franchising

The franchise sector in Mexico grew between 9 - 12% in 2011, continuing to be one of the most important sectors in the country's economic growth. Conservative estimates indicate that this sector will grow at least 8 percent in 2012.

Franchises in Mexico are regulated by Article 142 of the Industrial Property Law and Article 65 of its Regulations. Franchise agreements must be registered before the Mexican Institute of Industrial Property in order to be effective against third parties.

In January 2006, an amendment to the Mexican Franchise Regulations (Article 142) was published in the Mexican Official Gazette, stating a new definition of franchise, mandating requirements for franchise agreements, and providing new standards for pre-sale franchise disclosure.

Business opportunities for franchises encompass many sectors: food (fast food/casual restaurants), personal care services, education, and entertainment sectors for children, etc. Franchising in Mexico, as in any other country, requires a long-term commitment. Franchisors must commit human and financial resources, patience and time to make their concept succeed in the Mexican market.

For more information on franchising in Mexico, please see Chapter 4 of this Country Commercial Guide: Leading Sectors for U.S. Export and Investment – Franchising.

Direct Marketing

With the establishment of large international firms in Mexico and their emphasis in adopting similar marketing strategies to those of their international home base – in addition to more and better educated consumers with higher quality expectations – the marketing services industry has evolved into a more segmented and specialized sector offering U.S. companies a complete array of possibilities from which to choose.

Today, the choices firms have for promoting their products range from marketing campaigns through one-to-one contact at point-of-sale displays, to inserts distributed in monthly bills, to mass exposure through billboards or internet campaigns. Electronic media and Point of Sale Promotion (POP) are the most important vehicles of promotion.

In order to satisfy clients' demands, direct marketing has evolved combining different methods of promotion, including internet promotional campaigns. The most important promotional tools chosen by companies were direct mail and telemarketing.

Small and medium-sized U.S. companies that enter the Mexican market should work closely with their local distributor/representative in the creation of their marketing plan in order to have a strong presence in the market.

The leading association in Mexico that coordinates the activities of local/international marketing associations is CICOM (Confederation of the Industry for Marketing Communication)

Joint Ventures/Licensing

Given the flexibility of engaging in joint ventur e agreements, joint venturing and licensing are common approaches for U.S. firms interested in establishing a presence in Mexico. Although some Mexicans rely on verbal agreements when doing business, it is highly recommended to have a written joint venture agreement with your Mexican business partner. According to Mexican law, joint ventures are considered separate entities from their parent companies and must register separately to pay taxes.

To safeguard a license or patent against third parties, all licenses and patents in Mexico must be registered with the Mexican Institute of Intellectual Property (IMPI). Registering a license or patent entails a government review that can take up to twenty weeks. For more information on IMPI, please see the "Intellectual Property" section below.

Selling to the Government

The Mexican government purchases large volumes of raw material, repair parts, finished goods, and hired services, to execute important infrastructure and construction works. In 2012, Mexico's federal budget authorized by the Mexican Congress is USD $274.59 billion, of which 30% will be used for the purchase goods, 45% for services and 25% for construction services, according to official estimates.

Traditionally, the entities and enterprises with the largest purchasing budgets have been:

Public entities:
- Secretariat of Communications and Transport (SCT)
- Secretariat of Public Education (SEP)
- Treasury Department (SHCP)
- Secretariat of Health (SS)
- Secretariat of Public Security (SSP)
- Secretariat of National Defense (SEDENA)
- Navy (SEMAR)

Public enterprises:
- Mexican Petroleum (PEMEX)
- Federal Commission of Electricity (CFE)
- Mexican Social Security Institute (IMSS)

- The State Worker's Security and Social Services Institute (ISSSTE)

While maintaining a representative or office in Mexico is not a prerequisite to obtaining government contracts, it can simplify obtaining the information needed to prepare bid documents and support after-sales service and parts supply. It is strongly recommended that U.S. companies seeking government contracts work with a partner in Mexico. The U.S. Commercial Service can assist in identifying potential partners for U.S. companies. More information about these services can be found in Chapter 10.

U.S. firms are encouraged to carefully analyze with their representative the tender specifications. They may differ from entity to entity, depending on the value of operation, type of goods or services, budget limitations, etc. A bid will be disqualified if not received within the specified period of time. Stipulated bids can also be disqualified for not meeting technical details. Likewise, each tender includes a specific period of time for participants to ask questions. By paying attention to all the details, firms can avoid unnecessary disqualifications during the tender process. In some tenders, only written questions are permitted. Replies are given to all purchasers of the tender documents.

If a tender specifies a certain brand or gives preference to a supplier, a complaint can be filed with the General Directorate of Complaints before the contract is awarded. Each bid should only consider the exact specifications listed in the tender. "Additional solutions" and/or specifications not listed will disqualify the bid.

Finally, U.S. firms should communicate regularly with their Mexican representative and fine-tune all details related to the required documents. There have been numerous cases of disqualification based upon seemingly insignificant failures on the part of bidders to comply with tender regulations and procedures to the letter of the law.

Distribution and Sales Channels

Mexico has an adequate transportation network that is being modernized. The main land-border crossings with the United States are: Nuevo Laredo, Ciudad Juarez, Piedras Negras, Mexicali, and Tijuana. Tijuana is the world's busiest border crossing. However, the greatest value of goods pass through the Laredo/Nuevo Laredo land-border crossing, where approximately 60% of all U.S.-Mexican trade clears customs. The Government of Mexico and some state governments are trying to promote other border crossings, in order to decrease the concentration in Laredo and to offer future options to the increasing commercial traffic between the two countries.

Mexico has a modern highway system, primarily comprised of toll roads connecting the main industrial areas located in the Mexico City-Guadalajara-Monterrey triangle. Outside this area, road transportation is fair-to-poor. However, the Mexican government has enacted an aggressive program to improve Mexico's infrastructure, giving priority to the construction of new highways and modernizationof existing roads to create an efficient road network across the nation.

The main maritime ports are Altamira, Tampico, Veracruz and Progreso on the Gulf Coast of Mexico, and Ensenada, Lazaro Cardenas, Manzanillo and Puerto Madero on the Pacific Coast. All these ports have the infrastructure and equipment to facilitate intermodal, door-to-door merchandise transportation. The government's Infrastructure Program also includes important projects to modernize and expand existing ports and to build a new port in Punta Colonet Baja California, to attract container movement in transit from Asia to the United States. New multimodal corridors will be developed to connect Gulf and Pacific ports, and production and consumer centers, with NAFTA corridors.

Transportation-logistic services are expensive in Mexico: it is estimated that 8 to 15 percent of product cost in Mexico is related to logistics, compared to 5 to 7 percent in more developed countries.

According to 2011 figures provided by the Secretaría de Comunicaciones y Transportes, a large portion of Mexican products shipped domestically travel by road (about 61%), followed by maritime (27 %) and rail transportation (12 %). Within Mexico there were 584 million tons of transported goods; 355.5 million tons transported by highways, 157.7 million tons by ocean, 69.9 million tons by railroad, and .9 million tons transported by air. Given this distribution, the Mexican government is working to increase the volume of cargo using railroad transportation. North-South NAFTA trade has tripled over the past decade, straining the limit of Mexico's old transportation infrastructure. The Mexican government is fully committed to develop the necessary infrastructure and to promote private participation in the sectors that can help to make industry and exports more competitive.

Selling Factors/Techniques

In addition to developing strong working relationships with Mexican partners, it is highly recommended that U.S. firms use Spanish-language materials and speak Spanish whenever possible while doing business in Mexico. Hiring local staff can help facilitate these relationships and provide U.S. companies with insight on selling to the Mexican market.

Electronic Commerce

E-commerce between organizations and companies, either business to business (B2B) or government to business (G2B), has been developing much faster than e-commerce with consumers (B2C). Companies and the Mexican Government are investing heavily in their IT infrastructure to promote e-commerce between clients, suppliers, government, and individuals. Given that this market will grow in the future, there are great opportunities for suppliers of specialized and segmented solutions based on economic activity. The biggest market is enterprise solutions to help companies integrate and automate their communications within their organizations as well as with business partners (clients and suppliers).

Geographically, the three largest cities represent the highest density of Internet users in the country. Mexico City, Guadalajara, and Monterrey have over 50% of the 33 million Internet users in Mexico. The most sought after products and services by Internet users are the purchase of plane tickets, computers, show tickets, online bank transactions, and government services.

The increased use of e-commerce by government, companies, and individuals is due to significant increases in online transaction security mechanisms. There are laws and government agencies that focus on online fraud, piracy, and data protection.

Trade Promotion and Advertising

U.S. Commercial Service Mexico provides on-line advertising for U.S. and Mexican companies under the Business Service Provider (BSP) and Featured U.S. Exporter (FUSE) programs. For more information:

U.S. Commercial Service Mexico BSP Directory: http://export.gov/mexico/businessserviceproviders/index.asp

U.S. Commercial Service Mexico FUSE Directory: http://www.buyusa.gov/mexico/oportunidades denegociosconlosestadosunidos/index.asp

In order to have a better understanding of the Mexican market, it is also important to participate in industry trade events, seminars, and/or conferences in Mexico. Participating in such events gives you the opportunity to talk to suppliers, industry experts, and end users. It also provides business exposure and brand recognition.

A listing of trade shows in Mexico can be found at:
Mexico City:
http://www.biztradeshows.com/mexico/mexico/

Guadalajara:
http://www.biztradeshows.com/mexico/guadalajara/
Monterrey:
http://www.biztradeshows.com/mexico/monterrey/

Pricing

U.S. exporters should look carefully at import duties,
brokers' fees, transportation costs,
and taxes to determine if the product/service can be priced
competitively. U.S.
companies shipping goods not made in the United States
could be subject to duties.
For more information about import duties go to chapter 5.

Value Added Tax (IVA):
Mexican Customs collects a value-added tax (IVA) from
the importer on foreign transactions upon entry of the
merchandise into Mexico. This IVA is assessed on the
cumulative value consisting of the U.S. plant value (f.o.b.
price) of the product(s), plus the inland U.S. freight charges,
and any other costs listed separately on the invoice such as
export packing, insurance, plus the duty, if applicable. The
IVA is 11% for products exported to the "border zone,"
defined as 20 km from the U.S.-Mexico border. For final
shipping points other than the border zone, a 16% IVA is
charged. The importer will pay other fees for such services
as inland Mexico freight, warehousing, and custom
brokerage fees, if applicable. The IVA typically is
recovered at the point of sale when the product is sold. The
IVA is a pass-along tax. It is ultimately paid by the end-
user. Each time the product is sold the buyer is charged the
IVA. If resold, the company will then be reimbursed. Sales
of real property (real estate) within the border zone are
taxed at the 16% IVA rate.

Sales Service/Customer Support

Service and price are extremely important to Mexican
buyers. In many industries the decision to select a supplier
depends on the demonstrated commitment to service after

the sale has been made. This has been the most effective tool that third country manufacturers, have used to penetrate the market. They offer to have their maintenance personnel at the clients' plant in no more than 48 hours after a service call is made.

Mexican customers demand uniform quality control, compliance with international standards, productivity, lower production costs, just-in-time deliveries, and above all, reliable local service and maintenance programs. This last factor has become, in many instances, even more important than pricing or financing. Many Mexican firms employ English-speaking staff, but it is a good idea for the U.S. company to employ Spanish-speaking sales representatives. Providing appropriate training, product support, and timely supply of spare parts is critical for success. The U.S. exporter should also schedule annual visits of Mexican personnel to the U.S. companies for training. All Mexicans traveling to the United States for training or other business purposes need a visa – more information on the visa process is provided in Chapter 8. Another factor to consider is financing, as credit from Mexican banks is limited and when available can be quite high.

Protecting Your Intellectual Property

Several general principles are important for effective management of intellectual property rights in Mexico. First, it is important to have an overall strategy to protect IPR. Second, IPR is protected differently in Mexico than in the United States. Third, rights must be registered and enforced in Mexico, under local laws. Companies may wish to seek advice from local attorneys or IP consultants. The U.S. Commercial Service's Business Service Provider program has a list of local lawyers.

It is vital that companies understand that intellectual property is primarily a private right and that the U.S. government generally cannot enforce rights for private individuals in Mexico. It is the responsibility of the rights' holders to register, protect, and enforce their rights where relevant, retaining their own counsel and advisors. While the U.S. Government is willing to assist, there is little it can do if the rights holders have not taken the fundamental steps necessary to securing and enforcing their IPR in a timely fashion. Moreover, in many countries, rights holders who delay enforcing their rights on a mistaken belief that the U.S. Government can provide a political resolution to a legal problem may find that their rights have been eroded or abrogated due to doctrines such as statutes of limitations, laches, estoppel, or unreasonable delay in prosecuting a law suit. In no instance should U.S. Government advice be seen as a substitute for the obligation of a rights holder to promptly pursue their case.

It is always advisable to conduct due diligence on partners. It is recommended to negotiate from the position of your partner and give your partner clear incentives to honor the contract. A good partner is an important ally in protecting IP rights. It is recommended to keep an eye on your cost structure and reduce the margins (and the incentive) of would-be bad actors. Projects and sales in Mexico require constant attention. Work with legal counsel familiar with Mexican law to create a solid contract that includes non-compete clauses and confidentiality/non-disclosure provisions.

It is also recommended that small and medium-sized companies understand the importance of working with trade associations and organizations to support efforts to protect IPR and stop counterfeiting. There are a number of these organizations including:
   - The U.S. Chamber of Commerce
   - The American Chamber of Commerce in Mexico
   - National Association of Manufacturers (NAM)
   - International Intellectual Property Alliance (IIPA)
   - International Trademark Association (INTA)
   - The Coalition Against Counterfeiting and Piracy
   - International Anti-Counterfeiting Coalition (IACC)

- Pharmaceutical Research and Manufacturers of America (PhRMA)
- Biotechnology Industry Organization (BIO)
- Institute for the Protection of Intellectual Property and Legal Commerce (IPPIC)
- Mexican Association of Research Pharmaceutical Industries (AMIIF)
- Mexican Association of Phonogram Producers (AMPROFON)
- Motion Picture Association of America (MPAA)
- Business Software Alliance (BSA)

IPR Resources:
A wealth of information on protecting IPR is freely available to U.S. rights holders. Some excellent resources for companies regarding intellectual property include the following:
- For information about patent, trademark, or copyright issues -- including enforcement issues in the U.S. and other countries -- call the STOP! Hotline: 1-866-999-HALT or register at: www.StopFakes.gov
. - For more information about registering trademarks and patents (both in the U.S. as well as in foreign countries), contact the U.S. Patent and Trademark Office (USPTO) at: 1-800-786-9199.
- For more information about registering for copyright protection in the US, contact the U.S. Copyright Office at: 1-202-707-5959.
- For information on obtaining and enforcing intellectual property rights and market-specific IP Toolkits visit:
www.StopFakes.gov. This site is linked to the USPTO website for registering trademarks and patents (both in the U.S. as well as in foreign countries), the U.S. Customs & Border Protection website to record registered trademarks and copyrighted works (to assist customs in blocking imports of IPR-infringing products) and allows you to register for Webinars on protecting IPR.

- The U.S. Commerce Department has positioned IP attachés in key markets around the world. To contact the official IP Attaché who covers Mexico, please email:

dorian.mazurkevich@trade.gov

The Commercial Specialist covering these issues may be reached at: Jesus.Gonzalez@trade.gov

IPR Climate in Mexico:
Mexico continues to suffer from rampant commercial piracy and counterfeiting. The Mexican government has committed to strengthening protection of IPR, and the relevant federal agencies are working in a more integrated and aggressive manner. Nonetheless, a number of barriers to effective enforcement remain, including legislative loopholes, the need for improved coordination with state and municipal governments, issuance of more deterrent penalties, lack of specific legislation on data protection, and widespread public acceptance of illicit commerce.Mexico is working closely with the U.S. government and other partners to address these and other areas of mutual concern.

Two different laws provide the core legal basis for protection of intellectual property rights (IPR) in Mexico -- the Industrial Property Law (Ley de Propiedad Industrial) and the Federal Copyright Law (Ley Federal del Derecho de Autor). Multiple federal agencies are responsible for various aspects of IPR protection in Mexico. The Office of the Attorney General (Procuraduría General de la Republica, or PGR) has a specialized unit that pursues criminal IPR investigations. The Mexican Institute of Industrial Property (Instituto Mexicano de la Propiedad Industrial, or IMPI) administers Mexico's trademark and patent registries and is responsible for handling administrative cases of IPR infringement. The National Institute of Author Rights (Instituto Nacional del Derecho de Autor) administers Mexico's copyright register and also provides legal advice and mediation services to copyright owners who believe their rights have been infringed.

Mexico Customs Service (Aduana México) plays a key role in ensuring that illegal goods do not cross Mexico's borders. More information may be obtained at: http://www.impi.gob.mx/wb/impi_en/Home/_lang/en

Mexico is a signatory of at least fifteen international treaties, including the Paris Convention for the Protection of Industrial Property, NAFTA, and the WTO Agreement on Trade-related Aspects of Intellectual Property Rights.Although Mexico signed the Patent Cooperation Treaty in Geneva, Switzerland in 1994, which allows for simplified patent registration procedure when applying for patents in more than one country at the same time, it is necessary to register any patent or trademark in Mexico in order to claim an exclusive right to any given product. A prior registration in the United States does not guarantee its exclusivity and proper use in Mexico, but serves merely as support for the authenticity of any claim you might make, should you take legal action in Mexico.

An English-language overview of Mexico's IPR regime can be found on the WIPO website at: http://www.wipo.int/wipolex/en/profile.jsp?code=MX

Although a firm or individual may apply directly, most foreign firms hire local law firms specializing in intellectual property. The U.S. Commercial Service maintains a list of such law firms in Mexico at: http://export.gov/mexico/businessserviceproviders/index.as p?bsp_cat=80120000

Due Diligence

U.S. firms are strongly advised to conduct due diligence on a Mexican firm or individual before entering in any type of agreement. In Mexico's larger cities, it is possible to find a local consulting or law firm that can find information on a firm or individual. Also, local chambers and associations can assist U.S.firms in locating economic reports on a particular firm.

There are only a few private firms that conduct due diligence countrywide. U.S. firms should know that the U.S. Commercial Service has a service called International Company Profile (ICP) that can be ordered from our domestic U.S. Export Assistance Centers or our offices in Monterrey, Guadalajara, and Mexico City. The ICP is a report in English that includes financial and commercial information on a Mexican firm.

Local Professional Services

U.S. Commercial Service Mexico offers a wide variety of business services listed at: http://export.gov/mexico/businessserviceproviders/index.asp

Additionally, the following associations can be helpful for U.S. firms seeking more information on professional services:

The Mexican Association of Accounting Firms: http://www.amcp.org.mx

The Mexican Association of Electrical and Electronic Communications Engineers: http://www.amicee.org.mx

Mexican Association of Information-Technology Industries:

http://www.amiti.org.mx

The Mexican Association of Insurance Institutions: http://www.amis.com.mx

The National Auto-Freight-Transport Chamber: http://www.canacar.com.mx

The National Chamber of Consulting Companies: http://www.cnec.org.mx

U.S./Mexico Border Trade Initiative

Mexico's maquiladora and manufacturing export industry is the country's largest foreign currency income source, exceeding petroleum and tourism. As the U.S. and Mexican economies experience further integration, the more than 5,000 maquiladora plants throughout Mexico, 60% of which are located along the U.S.-Mexico border, will have an ongoing need to source quality inputs, equipment and services from U.S. industry.

The proximity of the U.S./Mexico border offersa cost-effective market entry opportunity, particularly for New to Export and New to Market companies. The U.S./Canada and U.S./Mexico borders are often the first step for companies breaking in to the international market given the accessibility and proximity the border economies afford.

In an effort to better assist U.S. businesses tap into the excellent sales opportunities offered by the maquiladora and manufacturing export industry, the Commercial Service created the Border Trade Initiative (BTI). The BTI extends the strong trade promotion programs that already exist throughout Mexicoto include the significant manufacturing clusters in the Mexican states bordering California, Arizona, New Mexico and Texas. The BTI offers matchmaking services, hands-on border programs, special events, market research and other tools to help U.S. businesses succeed along the border in this important growing market.

U.S. exporters are reminded that the border region also offers a myriad of export opportunities in other areas such as smart border technologies, security products and services, and technologies of interest to government customers such as waste management, energy savings solutions, and public safety products, to name a few.

In 2009 the BTI's border presence was enhanced by the opening of the first Export Assistance Center in El Paso Texas. This office provides direct assistance to U.S. companies in Texas, and also assists them in the neighboring state of Chihuahua. The El Paso Office has developed innovative methods of putting U.S. sellers together with maquiladora and manufacturing export industry buyers in Chihuahua (given the security challenges in this border region through export webinars in industry specific sectors). Similar programs also exist in Arizona and California.

Chapter 4: Leading Sectors for U.S. Export and Investment

Agribusiness

Overview:
Mexico is among the top 15 world leaders in the agribusiness industry with 27,300 hectares of permanent cropland. Mexico is also 10th in the world in terms of meat production, providing a total of 4,911 metric tons of red meat alone. For poultry production, Mexico is rated 3rdglobally.

2010 was a very dynamic year with an increase of 5.8% in the production of Mexico's 50 most important crops, which represents 86% of the total national agricultural production.

The sub-sectors that registered the most dynamic growth are: corn production with an increase of 17.6%, beans had an increase of 17.9 %, dairy sector had an increase of 1.5%, and cattle 2.1%.

The growing agribusiness sector demands modern agricultural machinery, more efficient technology, fertilizers, enhanced pesticides to protect crops, animal feed, and packaging equipment.

Best Prospects/Services

The agribusiness industry in Mexico is a sector with continuous expansion and an average annual growth of 2%. It is also responsible for 9% of the nation's foreign direct investment. The government's investment plan has provided the sector with over US$700 million in the past 5 years.

Modern Agricultural Machinery: This particular sector presents suppliers with strong opportunities, as 70% of Mexican agriculture is still harvested through manual labor utilizing rudimentary tools. Less than 20% of croplands are irrigated, leaving crops dependent on seasonal rains or irrigation through mobile water pumps. Federal government infrastructure development programs have provided this sector with US$300 million for this purpose alone.

Fertilizers: Mexico has no national fertilizer industry which results in farmers either fertilizing their crops with traditional products or not fertilizing at all. During 2010, farmers and organizations continued to express their discontent with the high price of imported fertilizers. Affordable fertilizers have strong market potential for U.S. firms in the agricultural sector.

Pesticides: Pesticides is another sector with virtually no national competition, and with harvestable land increasing yearly, there is strong market demand. These products have also received heavy subsidies by the federal government for small producers.

Packaging Equipment: General packaging equipment has also had a very considerable increase in demand due to producers' desire to begin packaging their own products. This is the case for the poultry and meat processing industry. Exports require standardized packaging and labeling requirements, which needs advanced technology and machinery that is not produced in Mexico.

Opportunities

There is virtually no national competition for agribusiness technology and equipment since 90% of products in this sector are imported, presenting an enormous opportunity for U.S. firms. U.S. products are most often the first choice for Mexican companies due in large part to the U.S. product reputation for excellent quality, innovation, and efficiency.

The performance of the Mexican economy is one of the most important factors affecting future agribusiness related purchases. The large number of free trade agreements that Mexico signed has created a more open and globalized economy, affecting local producers' demand and ability to compete with international and subsidized products.

Resources

Secretaria de Agricultura, Ganadería, Desarrollo Rural, Pesca y Alimentación:
www.sagarpa.gob.mx/
Comisión Federal para la Protección contra Riesgos: Sanitarios
www.cofepris.gob.mx/
Asociación Nacional de Comercializadores de Fertilizantes:
www.anacofer.com.mx/
Administración General de Aduanas:
www.aduanas.sat.gob.mx
Asociacion Mexicana de Horticultura Protegida:
www.amhpac.org

Automative Parts and Supplies

Overview

Auto Parts Production for OEM and Aftermarket:

	2009	2010	2011	2012 (est.)
Total Market Size	58.6	69.4	80.2	80.8
Total Local Production	41.2	57.5	66.9	68.0
Local Exports	35.9	37.9	45.1	45.9
Total Exports to the US	32.3	27.7.	40.2	41.1
Total Imports	18.5	26.0	31.8	33.1
Total Imports from the US	10.4	16.9	18.4	18.2

Total Number of Vehicles – Automobiles and Trucks:

	2009	2010	2011	2012 (est.)
Total Units Produced	1,507,527	2,260,774	2,557,550	2,791,292
Total Units Sold in Country	754,918	820,406	905,886	990,175
Total Units Imported	730,000	848,000	873,440	898,440
Total Units Exported	1,223,333	1,859,517	2,143,879	2,427,879

Total Value Vehicles – Automobiles and Trucks:

	2009	2010	2011	2012 (est.)
Mexican Exports of Vehicles to the US	878,742	1,277,184	1,440,481	1,447,425
Mexican Imports of Vehicles to the US	2,351	3,122	3,215	3,308

Mexico ranks as the 8th largest vehicle producer in the world, and the automotive sector accounts for 17.6 percent of Mexico's manufacturing sector and 3 percent of its national GDP contribution. There are currently nine manufacturers in Mexico including General Motors, Chrysler, Ford, Nissan, Fiat, Renault, Honda, Toyota, and Volkswagen. This manufacturing base produces 42 brands in 20 manufacturing plants. Nissan and Daimler are considering opening another manufacturing plant in Mexico to increase passenger car production. Nissan, GM, Volkswagen, and Honda plan to increase their production in Mexico. Fiat and Mazda are opening up plants for vehicle production in Mexico.

Mexico produces more than 2.5 million cars on a yearly basis. 83 percent of its production is devoted to exports and the remaining 17 percent for the domestic market. The National Auto parts Industry Association (INA) reported a significant increase in the auto parts industry from 2011 to 2012 as per estimates.

In 2011, the Mexican automotive industry experienced a 13.1% percent growth of local vehicle production due to higher demand, domestically as well as in the United States and other markets. The countries that Mexico exports to include: United States (64%); Canada (7%); Latin America (15%); Asia (2%), Europe (10%) and others (1%). Mexican vehicle sales in 2011 increased 10.4% compared with 2010. Market realities have led to new trends in car manufacturing, including smaller car sizes and increased fuel efficiency.

The aftermarket is expected to increase, as Mexico imposed new duties and requirements on the importation of used vehicles since 2009. As a result, repairing and maintenance of used vehicles will require varied parts. In addition, other opportunities exist for U.S. exporters of spare parts, equipment and new technologies oriented to reduce costs and time. Parts equipment and first and second-tier components from the United States might experience an increase in exports as auto production increases in Mexico.

The economic outlook for 2012 is conservative. Mr. Oscar Albin Santos, President of the National Auto Parts Industry expressed that the auto parts industry might report a production increase of one percent, an import increase of six percent and auto part export decrease of 4% by the end of 2012.

Furthermore, Eduardo Solis, Chairman of the Mexican Auto Association, acknowledged that the industry's situation remains linked to the economy and financial environment and forecasts a challenging 2012. To increase the demand in new car sales, the industry and the government will have to work on other strategies to target niches in the domestic market. The industry is currently working with the government to reduce taxes for purchasing a car, trade-in car replacement programs, among others. Despite the slow growth in demand and production, some automotive companies announced large investments in Mexico last year. This is due to Mexico's advantage in low labor costs and recent technological development in the auto industry through design centers. In addition, companies are looking for lower manufacturing and export costs.

Best Prospects/Services

The greatest opportunities include: spare and replacement parts for gasoline and diesel engines, electrical parts, collision repair parts, gear boxes, drive axles, catalytic converters, and steering wheels. In the first and second-tier supply chain sector, opportunities include: OEM parts and components, precision assembly devices, machined parts, hybrid vehicle components,suspension systems, and pre-assembly components such as small and progressive stampings. Other products in demand include electronic components, specialized tooling, systems that eliminate waste and green technologies such as new combustion systems to reduce gas emission and oil consumption.

Opportunities

Despite the economic recovery, lack of financing, high interest rates and competition, the market has become more price-sensitive. In Mexico, 50 percent of new cars are purchased on credit. Because of the credit shortage, new car sales have decreased and many consumers choose to maintain their vehicles for a longer period of time. As a result, President Calderon eliminated the ownership tax imposed to consumers effective Dec 31, 2011, with the exception of luxury vehicles. It is now the option of the Mexican state where the car is purchased to decide whether to charge this tax. Many Mexican states have decided not to charge this tax. This measure should stimulate the domestic market and the purchasing of new vehicles. In addition, OEMs located in Mexico will continue implementing strategic actions such as expanding their manufacturing base and upgrading their brand vehicles with new technologies to make them more efficient and affordable to consumers.

The large number of used vehicles being driven in Mexico provides opportunities for exports of repair equipment and replacementparts. Effective January 2009, Mexico imposed a 10 percent duty on imports of used vehicles, which was decreased to 3 percent only for the border zone in March 2009. In 2012 used cars 8-10 years old can be imported and in 2013 used cars6-8 years old can be imported. U.S. companies still face some barriers when exporting used cars to Mexico.

The most significant requirements include having a Certificate of Origin, and the 10 or three percent tariff based on a minimum estimated price, or "reference price" for the given year, make, and model of the car. Importers of used vehicles must post a guarantee representing any difference in duties and taxes if the declared customs value is less than the established reference price. Effective November 2011, the Mexican government set up a mandatory emission control standard for the import of used vehicles. To avoid red tape, U.S. exporters can attach emission control state certificates from Arizona, California, Texas and New Mexico as those states show very strict standards which are compliant with Mexican standard 041. Therefore, U.S. exporters are advised to work closely with their importers and customs brokers to ensure that all specific requirements are met.

Participation in Mexican automotive trade shows provides excellent opportunities to introduce new products and services in Mexico, after appointing regional distributors.

Education and Training Services
Overview

	2009	2010	2011	2012 (est.)
Number of Mexican Students	14,850	13,450	13,713	
% Change from Previous Year	0.1%	-9.4%	2%	2%

Mexico is the ninth country of origin for students studying in the United States, with over 13,500 Mexican students enrolled, primarily in undergraduate programs. Mexican students choose to study in the United States because of the strong ties between the countries, proximity, and the prestige of the higher education system in the United States. Approximately two percent of foreign students in the United States are from Mexico.

In recent years, most universities in Mexico, public and private, have started to develop international collaboration with foreign universities. In addition, the National Council of Science and Technology provides financial aid to graduate students who wish to study overseas. Student exchange will increase in the coming years because there is more information available, competitive education is growing and study and work experiences gained in foreign countries are more accepted in the business community.

There is also a demand for English language competency within Mexican higher education. Several Mexican private universitiesuse the TOEFL Institutional exam as a requirement for students in all fields of study to increase the knowledge of a second language in this competitive market. It is estimated that about 5% of Mexican ESL students travel abroad for intensive English programs.

Training Services:
Training opportunities in Mexico have increased in recent years. Private industry and local government entities have recognized that staff with the right balance of general and work specific competencies, personal attributes and interpersonal skills is increasingly required if Mexico wants to remain competitive in the global market.

Training in Mexico is basically divided into two segments: technical and executive training.

As technical training can be very specialized and unique according to the company's needs, some companies have a training department to deliver in-house programs. It is also common to partner with vocational schools to jointly develop technical courses.

In regards to executive training, private universities have developed "continuing education programs" as well as customized executive programs adapted to the needs of the industry. Soft skills training such as coaching programs are in great demand in Mexico.

Best Prospects/Services

•Short term ESL programs for students
•Student recruitment for engineering, business administration and environment/energy areas
•Corporate training programs in management, as well as executive-level language proficiency programs
•Dual-degree programs / collaborative programs in international business & management, engineering programs, environmental technology, robotics, nanotechnology, biotechnology, etc. (Undergraduate and graduate level)
•Technical programs

Opportunities
Mexican public and private colleges are focusing on alliances and agreements with foreign schools to provide joint programs, dual certification and exchange programs for students and professors. These programs have become more important as Mexico has become a key player in the world economy.

Also, technical programs for the automotive, health and services industries have strong potential in Mexico.

Energy Sector

Overview

Energy Market (USD Million):

	2010	2011	2012 (est.)	2013 (est.)
Total Market Size	9,781.5	10,159.3	10,543.7	10,944.9
Total Local Production	3,974.6	4,082.9	4,184.5	4,288.8

Total Exports	11,849.9	12,100.2	12,355.9	12,617.1
Total Imports	17,656.8	18,176.6	18,715.1	19,273.2
Imports from the U.S.	11,904.9	12,202.3	12,487.2	12,779.1
Exchange Rate: 1 USD	12.34	13.86	13.90	14.00

Oil and Gas Market (USD Million):

	2010	2011	2012 (est.)	2013 (est.)
Total Market Size	6,151.5	6,456.7	6,767.1	7,092.7
Total Local Production	1,924.6	1,991.9	2,051.7	2,113.3
Total Exports	1,329.9	1,369.8	1,410.9	1,453.2
Total Imports	5,556.8	5,834.6	6,126.3	6,432.6
Imports from the U.S.	3,954.9	4,093.3	4,216.0	4,342.5
Exchange Rate: 1 USD	12,34	13,86	13.90	14.00

Electric Power Sector:

	2010	2011	2012 (est.)	2013 (est.)
Total Market Size	3,630.0	3,702.6	3,776.6	3,852.2
Total Local Production	2,050.0	2,091.0	2,132.8	2,175.5
Total Exports	10,520.0	10,730.4	10,945.0	11,163.9
Total Imports	12,100.0	12,342.0	12,588.8	12,840.6
Imports from the U.S.	7,950.0	8,109.0	8,271.2	8,436.6
Exchange Rate: 1 USD	12.34	13.86	13.90	14.00

As illustrated in the energy market chart above, in 2012 and 2013, the demand for imported energy-related equipment and serviceswill increase by approximately 2.9 percent while U.S. exports to Mexico will grow by an estimated 2.3 percent during the same period of time.

With respect to the oil and gas chart above, in 2012 and 2013, the demand for imported oil and gas equipment and services will increase by approximately 4.9 percent while U.S. exports to Mexico will grow by an estimated 3.0 percent during the same period.

Oil and gas infrastructure will continue to be a priority for Mexico's federal government during the period 2012-2013. The state-owned energy company, Petroleos Mexicanos (PEMEX), has been granted a 2012 budget of USD 26.9 billion for new infrastructure and the maintenance of existing refineries, oil and gas pipelines, etc. (see "Opportunities" below)

On the electric power chart, in 2012 and 2013, the demand for imported equipment and services for this subsector will increase byapproximately 2.0 percent while U.S. exports to Mexico will grow an estimated 1.9 percent during the same period.

Best Prospects/Services

Energy sub-sectors: Oil and Gas (OGM),PEMEX will continue to make large investments in oil exploration and production in order to maintain falling production levels. PEMEX already relies heavily on imported products and services and is expected to continue to invest heavily indeveloping deepwater reserves as well as advanced extraction of maturing onshore fields. Also, natural gas capture at well heads is an opportunity for US companies.

Energy sub-sectors: Electric Power (ELP), Federal Electricity Commission (CFE) will continue to make large investments in infrastructure to increase the capacity of the electricity system, in automation to modernize the infrastructure of Mexico's Central Area, and in Smart Grid (an intelligent network is necessary to secure energy efficiency; however, the strategy and the projects related to Smart Grid are still being analyzed). CFE's priorities for the years to come are clean energy sources and energy efficiency.

Opportunities

A number of major projects will drive investment in the sector and offer US companies opportunities either as contractors, sub-contractors, or suppliers of equipment/technology:

Oil Exploration and Production:
53 exploration wells in the Chicontepec area with a budget of US$530 Million; 6 mature fields exploration wells in the

North Region with a budget of US$220 million 10 deep water exploration projects (including the Perdido Area) with a budget of US$300 million
40 offshore platforms on the Gulf of Mexico with a budget of US$ 1 billion.

Shale Gas Exploration:
10 wells in the State of Coahuila with a budget of US$150 million:
Pipe Rehabilitation and New Pipelines:
600 km natural gas pipeline project from Veracruz to Tamaulipas and Nuevo Leon with an estimated budget of US$700 million;
2,000 new kilometers of gas pipelines to link U.S. natural gas suppliers and Pemex gas pipelines system for States on the Gulf of Mexico and States on the Pacific.

Refineries:
Construction of the new refinery in Tula and reconfiguration of the Salina Cruz refinery.

Others: Pemex will increase the demand of Christmas Trees Control Systems (offshore); Wellheads; Drilling Rigs; Valves systems; Well shooting etc. The estimated budget is US$90 million.

Electrical Power System:

The most updated projects included in the long term investment program (Programa de Obras e Inversiones del Sector Eléctrico – POISE), can be found at www.sener.gob.mx/portal/Default.aspx?id=1453

The most updated CFE public tenders and contracts, can be found at www.cfe.gob.mx/proveedores/Paginas/Proveedores.aspx

Energy Efficiency:

The Sustainable Lighting Program (Programa de Luz Sustentable) from the Ministry of Energy, started in 2011 and will continue in 2012. This program aims to replace incandescent light bulbs with fluorescent light bulbs, which will represent 4,169 GWh of savings in energy consumption by the end of 2012. The official Mexican Standard (NOM) associated to this program, which establishes the minimum requirements for efficient light bulbs used in the residential, commercial, services, industrial, and public areas is NOM-028-ENER-2010. To learn more about this program, visit www.luzsustentable.gob.mx

Environmental Sector

Overview

Environmental Sector (USD Million):

	2010	2011	2012 (est.)	2013 (est.)
Total Market Size	5,892.0	6,091.5	6,284.8	6,452.5
Total Local Production	2,520.0	2,595.6	2,653.7	2,713.2
Total Exports	1,178.0	1,213.4	1,237.7	1,262.5
Total Imports	4,550.0	4,709.3	4,837.6	4,970.1
Imports from the U.S.	3,524.0	3,629.7	3,723.0	3,819.0
Exchange Rate: 1 USD	12,34	13,86	13.90	14.00

Water Technologies:

	2010	2011	2012 (est.)	2013 (est.)
Total Market Size	3,820.0	3,915.3	4,065.1	4,188.5
Total Local Production	1,225.0	1,255.6	1,286.9	1,319.0
Total Exports	765.0	787.9	803.7	819.8
Total Imports	3,360.0	3,477.6	3,581.9	3,689.3
Imports from the U.S.	2,010.0	2,086.6	2,149.1	2,213.6
Exchange Rate: 1 USD	12,34	13,86	13.90	14.00

The total market for the water and wastewater subsectors is estimated to grow by 3.8% from 2011 to 2012 and U.S. exports to Mexico are expected to increase by 2.9% during the same period.

The 2012 total budget from the Federal government to CONAGUA (National Water Commission) will reach over US$2.1 billion for new investment in water supply and wastewater treatment for the municipal and industrial sector. As a result of the new Public and Private Partnership Law approved bythe Mexican Congress, investment from private sector contractors in CONAGUA concessions is estimated to reach US$700 million in 2012. .

Environmental Technologies:

	2010	2011	2012 (est.)	2013 (est.)
Total Market Size	2,072.0	2,176.2	2,219.7	2,264.0
Total Local Production	1,295.0	1,340.0	1,366.8	1,394.2
Total Exports	413.0	425.5	434.0	442.7
Total Imports	1,190.0	1,231.7	1,255.7	1,280.8
Imports from the U.S.	1,514.0	1,543.1	1,573.9	1,605.4
Exchange Rate: 1 USD	12.34	13,86	13.90	14.00

Best Prospects/Services

The best prospects for US companies are in the sub-sectors of water resources equipment and services (WRE), Air Monitoring, and Solid Waste. See "Opportunities" below.

Opportunities

Water Purification Plants:
CONAGUA will invite companies to bid in the upgrading of 100 of the existing 631 plants. The estimated budget is US$35.5 million for plants in the states of Guerrero, Coahuila, Sinaloa, Tamaulipas, Zacatecas and Veracruz. CONAGUA plans to increase public access to water sanitations services from 49% coverage to 60% in 2012.

Desalination Plants:
CONAGUA is planning to invite private companies to bid on desalination plants for the cities of Hermosillo and Puerto Penasco in the State of Sonora as well as Los Mochis and Mazatlan in the State of Sinaloa. CONAGUA has indicated that the new desalination plants will be built using the new Public and Private Partnership Law as a framework.

Wastewater Treatment:
CONAGUA will invite companies to bid on the upgrading of 140, of the existing 2,029, municipal wastewater treatment plants mainly in the states of Aguascalientes, Chihuahua, Guanajuato, Jalisco, Nuevo Leon, Oaxaca, and Puebla, among others. The estimated budget is US$70 million. New plants will be built in the states of Puebla, Colima, Yucatan, Quintana Roo, State of Mexico, Nayarit, Guerrero, Colima, and others. CONAGUA has a budget of US$ 200 million for new plant construction.

In particular, CONAGUA plans to build a Atotonilco wastewater treatment plant in the State of Hidalgo. The private sector will finance 54% of the US$ 771 million price tag for what would be the largest wastewater treatment plant in Latin America.

Private companies in the cities of Tijuana, Mexicali, Cd. Juarez, Reynosa, Matamoros, Villahermosa, Leon, Irapuato, Queretaro, Toluca, Morelia, and Jalapa, among others, will invest US$80 million in upgrading their wastewater treatment plants to meet the wastewater discharge environmental standard. This will increase public access to water sanitation services from 49% in 2011 to 60% in 2012.

Waste Management:
Approximately 40 million tons of solid waste is generated every year in Mexico, from which approximately 88% corresponds to urban solid waste, and 12% corresponds to hazardous waste. In 2011, the federal government supported the construction of 113 landfills. Municipal, state, and federal authorities, with the support of the private sector, will continue to invest in solid waste management, particularly in projects to increase the capacity of sanitary fields and to construct new sanitary fields, to increase the capacity of recycling, to increase the use of organic waste, to transform PET, and to recover construction materials, among others.

Air Monitoring:
Mexico and the United States announced the Clean Air and Climate Change Coalition, with the objective of reducing emissions and contributing to the efforts against climate change. This initiative will allow improving air quality and protecting public health. Mexico has been monitoring the air in 70% of the national territory; the priority is to develop specific projects from all the states and their respective 1600 municipalities by 2013.

Franchising Sector:

Overview

The franchise sector in Mexico grew between 9 - 12% in 2011, continuing to be one of the most important sectors in the country's economic growth. Conservative estimates indicate that this sector will grow at least 8 percent in 2012.

Mexico is among the top ten nations in franchise development, due to the number of concepts operating in the market, strong legal framework as well as support from the government to continue developing new business opportunities.

According to the Mexican Franchise Association, Mexico has approximately 1,200 franchise concepts, including international brands, mainly from the United States. About 80 percent of the franchises operating in the country are Mexican franchisees, 10 percent are from the U.S., 3% from Spain, and the other 7% of the market is shared by Canada, Central & South America and Europe. Firms from other Latin American countries are finding Mexico as their best option to expand internationally, and are focused on exploring secondary markets.

The Mexican Franchise Association (AMF) has worked very closely with the Ministry of the Economy to develop the National Franchise Program (PNF). This program promotes the development of franchise concepts in Mexico with the goal of increasing employment and investment in the country. It provides opportunities to Mexican entrepreneurs to create or re-engineer a franchise concept, which not only supports growth and modernization of existing franchises, but provides support to investors looking to acquire international franchise concepts.

Due to the importance of the franchise industry to the Mexican economy, both in terms of job creation and percentage of GDP, the Mexican government has made numerous legislative changes to strengthen the legal framework for franchises. In 2006, the Mexican Congress amended the Law of Industrial Property to provide a clearer definition of a franchise, mandate requirements for franchise agreements, and provide standards for pre-sale franchise disclosures. These amendments help to protect franchisees who report abuse from franchisors when execut ing or terminating agreements. This has allowed further expansion of the franchise sector as the previous lack of regulation limited growth.

Franchising in Mexico, as in any other country, requires a long-term commitment. U.S. franchisors must commit human and financial resources, patience and time to make their concept succeed in the Mexican market.

U.S. franchises must be aware that since the Mexican market is dominated by local franchises, a requirement for a successful franchise concept in Mexico is to adapt, or customize, the concept and characteristics to Mexican tastes.

Best Products/Services

Although the food/restaurant sector in the franchise industry in Mexico has always been a very popular business model, the services sub-sector is rapidly growing. Services such as entertainment concepts for children and personal and home care services, have a great potential in the Mexican market.

Opportunities

Mexico is a diverse country that offers excellent business opportunities especially for U.S. franchise concepts due to the commercial ties between the countries and the recognition and acceptance of U.S. brands by the Mexican population. Low cost investment franchise concepts will be in demand in the next few years, as investors will be looking for innovative concepts to open in secondary markets.

Housing and Construction Services

Overview

	2010	2011	2012 (est.)
Total Market Size	70.28	83.37	86
Total Local Production	78.63	81.09	83
Total Exports	33.86	35.34	37
Total Imports	36.35	37.94	39
Imports from the U.S.	26.35	27.53	29

Construction

According to official figures presented by Mexico's Central Bank, the National Institute for Statistics and Figures (INEGI), the Mexican Chamber for the Construction Industry (CMIC), the National Chamber for Consulting Firms (CNEC), and the Secretariat of Treasury and Public Finance (SHCP), the Mexican construction industry grew 4.4% in 2011.

Mexico's goal is to be ranked in the top 30 of the world Economic Forum's Infrastructure Index. They have developed a new strategic plan that will steer the country into raising the coverage and quality of its infrastructure by 2012. According to that index, Mexico was ranked 71st out of 133 countries in 2009-2010, with the following rankings:

Airports: 56th, Railways: 66th, Ports: 82nd, Highways: 57th, and Telecommunications: 65th.

The aim of the National Infrastructure Plan (NIP) for 2012 is to increase economic growth as well as permanent job creation by developing transportation, communications, water and energy to convert Mexico into one of the main logistic platforms and promote regional development and tourism. Regarding the financial requirements for 2012, US$194.3 billion are split as shown below:

US$33.1 billion: Private Investment
US$8.7 billion: National Infrastructure Fund (FONADIN)
US$5.3 billion: National Development Bank (BANOBRAS)

US$147.2 billion: National Budget

This investment is not only to spur the economy, but also to address the lack of infrastructure investment projects in the past, and the importance of works to support the competitiveness of the country. The Mexican construction industry aims to grow 4.6% during the present year, based on the NIP for 2012. Key infrastructure projects sponsored by the government and large private projects developed and executed by local and foreign investors (shopping malls, retail stores, industrial plants, distribution centers, mixed-use buildings, housing and other small projects) will be the best opportunities for investment during 2012.

The total value of the construction sector in 2011 was USD $83 billion. Much of this (48%) was allocated to PEMEX investment projects, followed by the building of houses and multi-use buildings (16%), and then highway construction (12%). The Mexican states that received the majority of investment were Estado de Mexico (18%), Mexico City (17%), Nuevo Leon (14%), Jalisco (8%) and Veracruz (7%).

Housing:

Under the current administration all housing initiatives and projects throughout Mexico are considered to be a priority. All government levels in Mexico are working closely to strengthen the housing industry in order to solve Mexico's housing deficit of over 5 million units countrywide. All housing agencies, both government and private, are promoting projects and seeking private investment in order to counter the country's housing deficit.

The housing initiatives announced by President Calderón will impel the housing industry in the short and medium term. These initiatives will support Sare, Urbi, Ica, Ara, Geo and Homex, the largest housing developers, as they aim to accomplish the housing plans of the present Administration. Some of the initiatives are: a) Support the 6 million workers not affiliated with the two Mexican housing funds, Infonavit and Fovissste, b) A subsidy of USD $700 million for houses valued between US$12,000 and US$25,000, c) More subsidy for green housing projects (up to 20% of the mortgage), among others. Based on these initiatives, housing firms consider that their construction plans will grow 8 percent during 2012.

Inflation affected construction costs by nearly 9 percent in 2011, according to the Index of Prices to the Builders from the Banco de Mexico. An inflation rate of 5 percent is expected in 2012.

For U.S. firms interested in entering Mexico's construction industry, one of the best options is to sign a joint venture agreement with a Mexican housing developer or construction firm that is active in the housing industry. Mexican companies' knowledge of the market, and the labor and legal aspects involved in this industry is invaluable to U.S. firms.

Green Building:
Similar to other emerging economies, Mexico is moving towards "green" or friendlier environmental activities. The construction industry has embraced the green building movement. Mexico has joined the World Green Building

Council (WGBC). Mexico is learning from the European, Canadian and United States' best practices and occasional missteps to reap the cost and health benefits of green buildings. It also can show other countries how to use simple, moderate-cost strategies from its own longstanding building practices to achieve green building advantages. Mexico has a tradition of architecture that favors environmentally sensitive, small-footprint building practices and designs. However, policy efforts to promote green buildings are relatively new and generally focused on the housing sector. Mexico's National Housing Commission (CONAVI), INFONAVIT (the largest housing fund for workers in Mexico), the Mexican Chamber for the Construction Industry (CMIC), the National Chamber for Consulting Firms (CNEC), the National College for Architects, the Mexican Council for Sustainable Edification and the Association of Firms for the Saving of Energy on Construction and Buildings are documenting green practices and working to define criteria for green buildings and homes. Additionally, INFONAVIT has created a "green mortgage" program, supported bymandatory employer and employee contributions.

Although green construction in Mexico continues on a growth trend, the actual numbers for the sustainable construction remain small. Currently Mexico has only five buildings with LEED certification and over 80 in the LEED certification process. Nonetheless, rating programs, market surveys, and anecdotalevidence indicate tremendous growth in this field. Projects include real estate branches for tourism, marine, thematic and recreational parks, golf courses, residential areas and housing, town planning, and industrial and commercial. Without widespread performance data and agreed upon performance benchmarks for comparison, no method exists to determine precisely how many buildings are green. Like many other countries Mexico will continue supporting these green initiatives for the construction and sustainable development sectors. Several investors and developers are moving towards into the construction of green buildings, some of them will be LEED certified and others will be eco-friendly buildings.

Best Products/Services

Mexico offers solid sales opportunities for American manufacturers of housing and building materials. Materials with the best current sales potential are:

Description	HS Code	U.S. Market Share
AC Systems	841582	83%
Air filters for AC systems	842139	67%
Aluminum doors, windows and frames	761010	75%
Bulbs for incandescent lamps	701110	52%
Clear glass with UV protection and thickness over 6mm	700490	95%
Kitchen cabinets and fixtures	940340	25%
Prefab construction systems	940600	30%
Solar panels for lighting	854140	15%
Solar water heaters	841919	15%
Steel doors, windows and frames	730830	62%
Toilet articles of porcelain or china	691090	27%
Tubes and pipes – copper	741110	85%

Opportunities

Concessions, PEF (projects funded by the Federal Government), PPP's (private public partnerships), and Highway Assets (projects supported by FARAC funds), are the most utilized tools that the Mexican government is using to promote private investment in infrastructure projects. These projects are supported by the Mexican government funding institutions, as well as international funds such as BANOBRAS (National Public Works Bank), FONADIN (National Fund for Infrastructure Development), local and foreign banks, the North American Development Bank, Interamerican Development Bank, World Bank, OPIC, USTDA, ExIm Bank, and USAID.

In December 2012, Mexico approved a new Public-Private Partnership Law (PPP Law), which allows the government to enter into infrastructure and service provision contracts with private companies for up to 40 years. The Public-Private Partnership Law provides more legal certainty to private investors through an equal distribution of risk. This harmonizes existing state public-partnership models into one federal law. All investors will be allowed to participate in bidding processes, except for some restricted sectors, according to the existing Foreign Direct Investment Law.

The largest housing developers listed on Mexico's stock market announced an expected 8% income growth in 2012. Representatives from Mexico's main housing stakeholders (ARA, GEO, HOMEX, URBI, SARE and ICA) said that the housing sector in Mexico will continue its growth and that the best market in the housing industry exists for houses between USD $26,000 and $50,000. Additionally, the low-income housing between $12,000 and $25,000 USD will grow due to Federal, State and Municipal incentives to support this sector of the Mexican population.

Although the housing sector will not be affected, the global economic slowdown and the electoral year will probably hit other segments of the construction industry in Mexico. Estimated effects include the delay or postponement by the Mexican government of some major infrastructure projects due to the increased cost of products, including cement, steel bar, and glass.

Internet and IT Services

Trends in the Internet Markets:

	2009	2010	2011 (est.)
Total Market Size	2,074	2,302	2,558
Total Local Production	2,074	2,302	2,558

Trends in the IT Services:

	2009	2010	2011 (est.)
Total Market Size	2,484	2,957	3,331
Total Local Production	2,691	3,203	3,608
Total Exports	828	985	1,109
Total Imports	621	739	832
Imports from the U.S.	250	298	337

The IT services & outsourcing market in Mexico continues to show great opportunities given the increased implementation and renovation of IT infrastructure in all types and sizes of organizations, both in the private and public sectors. Mexico is becoming an attractive market for U.S. technology productsin the IT services industry.

Further Mexico is becoming a stronger global player in the Business Process Outsourcing (BPO) markets, developing IT hubs around the country to offer IT, software development, call center, high-tech manufacture and engineering services to users in industrialized economies in North America and Europe. The Mexican market overall, suffered in 2009, but bounced back in 2010. It is estimated that the IT and telecom market in Mexico will be worth over US$37.2 billion, whereas in 2008 it was worth almost US$40.4 billion.

Mexico is following a strong trend to have a service-centric IT industry where most technologies will be offered under a service contract or lease. We are seeing a growing interest of Software as a Service (SaaS) or Infrastructure as a Service (IaaS), and Platforms as a Service (PaaS). The main driver for users to support this new business model is cost reduction in areas that are not mission critical and represent cost without value added and offer commodity services. Due to the cost reduction attribute of IT services, this segment of the industry was the least affected in 2009 with the economic downturn.

Best Products/Services
Demand of IT services will grow in to service contracts in different areas such as:
- Security Services
- Training (bundled with an overall solution)
- Tailored Software Applications
- Leased Infrastructure (NOCs, SOCs).
- Wireless Applications (mainly focused on mobile broadband, such as TV)
- Maintenance

- Consulting and IT/Systems Integration
- CATV Network Applications

•Business Intelligence Software

As mentioned above, technology as a service will be the predominant business model for users and suppliers. SaaS, IaaS, and PaaS will provide the best opportunities. Also, the general technology trends are present in Mexico where new opportunities will arise. These are:
- •Web 2.0
- •Social Networks
- •Cloud Computing and Network Terminals Using Web- Based Applications
- •Virtualization
- •Online Advertising
- •Mobile Broadband
- •Green IT
- •IT & Healthcare

Opportunities

The main opportunities for IT solutions (products and services) are those sectors that are intensifying the use of IT and include: healthcare, transportation, security, manufacturing, energy, retail and financial services. Both public and private organizations are good targets of opportunity.

Currently the strongest driver for IT is government at every level (local, state and federal). They seek solutions to increase transparency, effectiveness and communication with citizens. Governments also have relatively large budgets to plan, design and implement technological tools. Most public agencies will seek to forego capital investments (CAPEX) and identify IT service providers that can integrate turn-key solutions under a lease contract.

Small and Medium size Enterprises (SMEs) are also represent a growing opportunity given that they seek much simpler solutions and thus, require less maintenance and administrative handling of accounts.

IT Healthcare

<u>Overview</u>

The market for IT in the healthcare sector in Mexico is an emerging market as most health care institutions have recentlystarted the process of identifying technologies that can help them to be more efficient and competitive in the services they offer. Currently, the technologies that are more popular in the sector are those for patient c ontrol, electronic file, supplies inventory control, pharmacy inventory and services control, and security systems.

Potential clients for IT in the health care sector are mainly the large hospitals in the public and private sector with resources to purchase sophisticated technologies to automate patient service and administrative and supplies control systems. In the public sector there are 1,169 hospitals of which, 194 are highly specialized medical units. In the private sector, of the 3,140 hospitals, only 80 have over 50 beds and offer highly specialized medicine. Most of the hospitals offering specialty health care services are located in medium and large Mexican cities. There are also some medium sized private hospitals that offer specialty services and focus on high income, insured patients. These hospitals also represent potential users of IT health care applications.

Based on surveys and market information, the private consulting company Select estimated that in 2011, the Mexican healthcare sector invested approximately US$ 488 millions in IT systems. This market is expected to continue growing, as automating technologies increase in the Mexican healthcare sector.

<u>Information Technology</u>

IT in health care is a growing trend in Mexico, mainly with private hospitals and clinics. Some of the biggest and more recognized hospitals are focusing on implementing the

Electronic Health Record, HER (Expediente Clínico Electrónico) as well as other automation and control systems. These hospitals are also evaluating technologies and integrated systems that can provide real-time information and communication with staff and patients.

Depending on the size of the hospital, the average cost to upgrade IT platforms US$10 million. Clinics focus more on productivity and efficiency systems for billing and data transmission.

IMSS (Mexican Institute of Social Security) and ISSSTE (Institute of Social Security and Services for Public Employees) are also upgrading their systems to manage and improve the network of hundreds of clinics, huge medicine inventories, appropriate billing systems and supplier relationships. Other government health care institutions are also seeking improvements in their operations, including greater transparency, efficiency, and effective use of resources.

Best Products/Services

Products and systems that offer opportunities in the market include:
- Automation hardware and software
- Billing systems
- Data protection systems
- Electronic Health Record (EHR)
- EPR systems (Enterprise Resource Planning)
- Green IT-systems to reduce energy consumption
- Hands-free and wireless communication mobile devices
- Imaging transferring systems
- Medical data exchange solutions
- Mobile devices for medical use
- Nursing systems
- Patient tracking systems
- Real-time database update accessible from multiple devices

Opportunities

Main opportunities are found with the private hospital networks, mainly with the large groups such Grupo Angeles and Star Médica. Other private hospitals are also good targets for innovative communications and automation solutions. Most private hospital groups are developing their 5-year tech innovation plan.

The government sector also provides specific solutions with the public social service and healthcare institutions (IMSS, ISSSTE, and Pemex, State social security and health services). Given the more limited budget in the public sector, these institutions are seeking solutions that can effectively manage their resources such as medicines, clinics, personnel, facilities, and budgets.

Medical Devices

Overview

Mexico imported medical equipment, instruments, disposable and dental products worth US $3.5 billion in 2010. This represented 90 percent of the medical equipment and instrument market and 2 percent of the disposables. Of these imports 57 %, or US$ 2 billion, were of U.S. origin. The main foreign suppliers of medical devices are Belgium, Brazil, Canada, China, France, Germany, Israel, Italy, Japan, Netherlands, South Korea and UK.

U.S. medical products are highly regarded in Mexico due to their high quality, after sales service, and price point compared to competing products of similar quality. Consequently, U.S. medical equipment and instruments have a competitive advantage and are in high demand in Mexico.

Public health care institutions account for 70 – 80 percent of total medical services provided nationwide whileprivate health care institutions cover approximately 25-30 percent of the Mexican population, including 32 million people with private medical and accident insurance. In 2007, Mexico had 3,140 accredited private hospitals, of which only 80 had more than 50 beds and the capacity to offer highly specialized services.

Best Products/Services

Best prospects include the following:

- Anesthesia equipment
- Defibrillators
- Electrocardiographs
- Electroencephalographers
- Electro surgery equipment
- Gamma ray equipment
- Incubators
- Lasers for surgery
- MRI equipment
- Patient monitors
- Respiratory therapy equipment
- Suction pumps
- Ultrasound equipment
- X ray equipment

Key factors in order to successfully compete are quality, after sales service, warranty and price.

Opportunities & Challenges

Most large public and private hospitals are regularly seeking the most modern and highly specialized medical devices. Some medium and small private hospitals with limited budgets buy used or refurbished equipment. However, public hospitals by law, cannot buy used or refurbished products. In order to reduce costs many public and private hospitals are outsourcing parts of their medical treatment services to companies that offer "integral surgery services". This is delivered as a "pay per event", which includes all the necessary products required to perform a surgery. As such, hospitals are able to avoid big capital investments in materials, pharmaceuticals, and instruments, and at the same time gain access to some of the most modern specialized surgical equipment.

Most medical and health care products need to be registered with the Mexican Secretariat of Health (SSA) prior to sale or use in Mexico. In addition, foreign medical device manufactures require a legally appointed distributor/representative in Mexico responsible for the product and registration process. Lastly, there can be delays in receiving registration/marketing approvals from COFEPRIS.

Packaging Equipment

Overview
Packaging Goods Statistics (metal, plastics, glass, wood, cardboard):

(Production)	2009	2010	2011	2012
Estimated Total Market Size	$10,135.1	$10,795.5	$11,227.3	$11,620.3
Estimated Total Local Proudction	$9,022.0	$9,706.4	$10,094.7	$10,448.0
Total Exports	$1,156.5	$1,319.5	$1,372.3	$1,420.3
Total Imports	$2,269.6	$2,408.6	$2,504.9	$2,592.6
Imports from the U.S. (according to Mexico)	$103.0	$99.9	$103.9	$107.5
Imports from the U.S. (according to the U.S.)	$119.7	$126.4	$131.5	$136.1

In 2010, the packaging production industry represented 1.5% of Mexico's national gross domestic product (GDP), 5.2% of the industrial sector GDP and 8.5% of manufacturing GDP. The latest statistics show that total Mexican packaging production reached 9.1 million tons of containers and materials for a value of US$10.1 billion, of which US$2.5 billion was imported. According to reports from the Packaging Machinery Manufacturers Institute (PMMI), referring to HS Codes 842220 and 842290, Mexico is the second largest buyer of U.S. packaging equipment, only preceded by Canada.

In terms of equipment purchased for the packaging industry, Mexico fell two spots, from 6th to 8th, in 2010 among the world's top markets for packaging equipment. Imports of packaging equipment dropped 3% to equal US$478 million in 2010. The United States remained the second largest supplier (US$ 100 million) behind Italy (US$ 144 million) and closely followed by Germany (US$ 95 million), which increased sales by 5% from the previous year. In 2011, Mexico's market turned around and the country increased its imports of packaging equipment by at least 4%.

The Mexican packaging products market is very dynamic. According to AMEE, the breakdown in sub-sectors in 2010 is as follows:

The cardboard and paper packaging sectorrepresented 37.03 % of total sales in the industry. Sales value increased 17% compared to 2009.

The plastic packaging sector (bags, films, boxes, bottles, containers) represented 25.14% of all sales in the industry. It increased sales by 2.7%.

The metal packaging sector holds 20.62% of the industry grew 7.1%.

The glass-packaging sectorrepresented 16.77% of all sales in the industry and is expected to become a fast-growing sub-sector in Mexico. Sales value grew by 0.8%. This was one of the most prosperous sub sectors, especially considering that Mexico is the world's third largest beer producer and second largest soda consumer. The beer sector alone reported an increase by 5.3%, producing 3,704 million of bottles in 2010.

Wood packaging sector represents 0.45% of all sales in the industry, and is the only sub-sector in which local production is decreasing because of a shortage of wood. Nonetheless, imports of wooden products, mostly pallets, increased by 72.89%

Food processing accounts for 19% of Mexico's manufacturing GDP and also for 40% of sales in the packaging industry, making the food processing sector the biggest buyer of the packaging industry. The food processing sector demonstrated an average growth rate of 3.2% in 2010, compared to 2009. Mexico is currently the 6th largest soft beverage market in the world with estimated annual sales of US$11,501.7 billion in 2011 and a forecast of US$15,972.1 going forward to 2015.

The pharmaceutical market is also one of the major correlated industries, considered as the 9th largest one in the world and leader for Latin America; it represents almost 10% of the total packaging materials demand. And one of the largest buyer industries for packaging equipment, with an annual average growth rate of 7% in the last three years. Some of the international companies that have operations in Mexico are: Roche, Pfizer, Glaxo Smith Kline, Novartis, Schering Plough, Eli Lilly y Johnson and Johnson.

Cosmetics and Personal Care Products is the third most relevant sector /client for the packaging industry, with 10% of the overall demand for packaging equipment.

Opportunities

Mexico is striving to provide higher and higher quality in the packaging sector. The glass packaging industry has become the main focus for many companies because of its competitive prices as compared to plastic containers and its environmentally friendly manufacturing process.

Companies involved in food processing or even agribusiness (Tyson, BACHOCO, Driscolls, Sunny Ridge, etc) are demanding more and better packaging products, in most cases to help extend the shelf life of their products or to fulfill the marketing trends or requirements from major retailers such as Wal Mart.

With this trend in the packaging sector, machinery is more in demand. However, the United States has lost some of its market share to Mexico's first-ranked supplier Italy and now its closest competitor Germany. When asked why a Mexican company would prefer a European supplier (farther than the United States and pricier in Euros), some executives told FCS that it was because of flexibility in terms of adapting equipment to local needs, better after-sales service from centers located in Mexico, and availability of financing options. U.S. firms should keep these critical points in mind while continuing to take advantage of the American reputation for having the newest technologies, being located at a convenient distance, extensive trade relationship and NAFTA preferences. Despite Mexico's depreciation of the peso (hit a two year low in November 2011 against US dollar and Euro), over 85% of all new packaging equipment is imported, which represents an enormous opportunity for U.S. firms.

Plastic Materials/Resins

Overview

Mexico ranks as the 12th largest plastics consumer in the world, which accounts for 5.3 percent of the manufacturing sector and one percent of Mexico's GDP. According to the National Association of the Plastic Industry (ANIPAC), there are 4,102 plastic companies in Mexico. Out of that number, 60 percent are micro companies, 24 percent are small, 12 percent are medium-sized and four percent are large companies. ANIPAC also revealed that 42 percent of the companies are concentrated in the Metropolitan area (Estado de Mexico and Mexico City), 14 percent in Jalisco, 8.5 percent in Nuevo Leon and 3.4 percent in Baja California Norte. Mexico consumes around 5.3 million tons of plastic products each year and 4 million tons for raw materials. Direct plastic consumption per capita in Mexico is 48 kg a year.

Over the last six years, markets became more focused and so did the competition. The Mexican plastics industry underwent a long process of consolidation. Smaller companies merged with larger ones seeking to gain more market share as Asian competition grew stronger.

Productivity in Mexican plastics manufacturers has risen 56 percent over the last five years. The plastics industry has seen an average annual investment of more than $1 billion over the last 10 years, with $1.4 billion invested in 2011, a clear indication of the increased strength of this industry.

While there is an excess domestic supply of PVC, PET, and polystyrene, the limited supply of polyethylene and polypropylene means that the Mexican plastics industry has to import raw material from the U.S. and Canada, as seen in the following chart for the U. S. trade activity with Mexico.

Best Products/Services
The packaging segment remains the key growth driver. Amongst the individual plastic materials, the highest prospects can be found in Thermoplastics (PE, PP, PVC, PS, PET, ABS/SAN Nylon and Engineering Plastics); and Thermoset (PU, Epoxy, Melamine, Unsaturated PE, Phenolics and Poly Lactic Acid).

Specialized and reliable mold making, repair and maintenance are in moderate demand. Machine retrofitting activity is becoming outdated and manufacturers think it is a good time to invest in modernization

Opportunities

Despite the abundant crude oil reserve and a 20 million ton capacity for petrochemical product elaboration, Mexico continues importing millions of dollars in oil derivatives; this includes not only finished materials but also primary products that could be generated domestically. Mexico is exporting Ethylene and imports Polyethylene thus showing the need for polymerization technology.

Renewable Energy
Overview

Renewable Energy Market:

	2010	2011	2012 (est.)	2013 (est.)
Total Market Size	2,101.2	2,166.5	2,512.8	2,966.0
Total Local Production	317.8	325.7	334.4	343.3
Total Exports	318.6	328.9	339.5	350.4
Total Imports	2,102.0	2,169.7	2,517.9	2,973.1

| Imports from the U.S. | 865.7 | 901.4 | 1,050.7 | 1,240.8 |

(Figures listed in USD millions)

Wind Energy Market:

	2010	2011	2012 (est.)	2013 (est.)
Total Market Size	824.0	848.1	1,147.2	1,551.5
Total Local Production	110.0	112.7	116.0	119.5
Total Exports	120.0	123.6	128.5	133.6
Total Imports	834.0	859.0	1,159.7	1,565.6
Imports from the U.S.	341.3	354.9	479.1	646.8

(Figures listed in USD millions)

Solar Energy Market:

	2010	2011	2012 (est.)	2013 (est.)
Total Market Size	824.0	848.1	1,147.2	1,551.5
Total Local Production	110.0	112.7	116.0	119.5
Total Exports	120.0	123.6	128.5	133.6
Total Imports	834.0	859.0	1,159.7	1,565.6
Imports from the U.S.	341.3	354.9	479.1	646.8

(Figures listed in USD millions)

Hydro Energy Market:

	2010	2011	2012 (est.)	2013 (est.)
Total Market Size	260.8	272.8	283.6	294.8
Total Local Production	73.6	75.8	78.1	80.4
Total Exports	41.9	43.6	44.7	45.8
Total Imports	229.1	240.6	250.2	260.2
Imports from the U.S.	118.0	129.9	135.1	140.5

(Figures listed in USD millions)

Geothermal Energy Market:

	2010	2011	2012 (est.)	2013 (est.)
Total Market Size	185.5	190.5	197.3	204.3
Total Local Production	41.2	42.2	43.3	44.4
Total Exports	49.9	51.7	53.0	54.3
Total Imports	194.2	200.0	207.0	214.2
Imports from the U.S.	100.9	104.0	107.6	111.4

(Figures listed in USD millions)

Biomass Energy Market:

	2010	2011	2012 (est.)	2013 (est.)
Total Market Size	93.7	96.6	100.4	104.4
Total Local Production	10.8	11.2	11.5	11.8
Total Exports	9.8	10.1	10.4	10.7
Total Imports	92.7	95.5	99.3	103.3
Imports from the U.S.	47.3	49.7	51.7	53.8

(Figures listed in USD millions)

As illustrated in the tables above, the demand for imported renewable energy-related equipment and services will increase by approximately 4 percent in 2012 and 2013, while U.S. exports to Mexico will grow by the same amount in the same years. The only exception is wind power, which is the fastest growing renewable energy in Mexico at an estimated 35% growth in 2012 and 2013. Mexico grew from 3 MW of installed wind power capacity in 2005 to 1,108 MW in place by April 2012 and experts have defined a potential of at least 12,000 MW, which would reach 15% of the total energy generation by 2020.

Energy production and infrastructure will continue to be a priority for Mexico's federal government during 2012, the last year of President Calderon's administration. Given Mexico's proximity to the United States, the absence of import duties on U.S. exports to Mexico (as a result of NAFTA) and the lack of manufacturing capacity currently in Mexico's renewable energy industry, the market would likely be an area of distinct U.S. export competitiveness.

Best Prospects/Services

Energy sub-sectors: WindPower, Hydropower, Solar, Geothermal, and Biomass renewable energy sub-sectors continue to grow and represent opportunities for US exporters.

The industry's growth has been driven primarily by government targets for renewable energy and the availability of a world-class wind resource in southern Mexico and coastal states, particularly those close to the border with the United States, which matches California's demand for extra energy.. Mexico is modernizing at a fast pace and this is the right time to participate in this explosive growth. Additional efforts on sustainability include the governments of Mexico and the United States signing a Memorandum of Understanding in January 2012, outlining a program of technical collaboration to develop and expand Mexico's Low Emissions Development Strategy with funding of $70M for the following five years.

Opportunities

A number of major projects will drive investment in the sector and offer opportunities to US companies either as contractors, sub-contractors, or suppliers of equipment/technology. During the first months of 2012, 650 MW of new capacity will be launched with projects such as La Venta III & Oaxaca I, II, III & IV. Afterwards, the next planned renewable power projects are:

Project/Capacity	Technology	Timing
Cerro Prieto (5 MW)	Solar	Q3 2012
Sureste I (300 MW)	Wind	2012
Sureste II (300 MW)	Wind	2013
Sureste III (300 MW)	Wind	2015
Sureste IV (300 MW)	Wind	2016
Rumorosa I (100 MW)	Wind	2014
Rumorosa II (100 MW)	Wind	2014
Rumorosa III (100 MW)	Wind	2015

Security and Safety Equipment and Services

Overview

	2010	2011	2012 (est.)
Total Market Size	2,210	2,746	3,319
Total Local Production	1,892	2,232	2,567
Total Exports	1,462	1,554	1,647
Total Imports	1,780	2,068	2,399
Imports from the U.S.	590	744	930

(U.S. million dollars)

In Mexico, the year of 2011 had a strong recovery in the security and safety industry with an average market advance of 18%. However, the whole economy grew only 3.9%, a little less than expected by several lead financial institutions. The growth tendency for the sector in 2012 is positive and could be situated between 15-18% .The demand for security and safety products and services has expanded in all categories of the industry, but mainly in personal protection and perimeter surveillance/protection. Other residential and industrial security solutions represent leading market segments. Organization and citizens have increased their awareness to create security policies to keep their assets safe. The security market offers information and diverse solution for all type of consumers, but the sector has seen new players looking to enter the market.

The private sector considered 2011 a good year for the industry. Some segments were more dynamic than others, such as CCTV, alarms, perimeter and personal protection devices, and GPS applications, but the industry has maintained its place as one of the most dynamic industrial sectors in the country. The outlook for 2012 also has good perspectives; the economic forecasts are estimating an economic growth of around 3.2%.

Opportunities for government procurement contracts are also expected to continue throughout 2012. Federal and state governments are aware of the need to modernize their prison systems and reduce the saturated level of inmates. However, such projects will face moderate budgets, even though theyare urgent. The upcoming presidential elections may delay their approved budgets. At the same time, command operation centers around the country were installed in the last two years and may represent business opportunities for maintenance, integration services and improvement projects. Some other state governments will be following this tendency to be more effective in terms of providing better public security.

In 2011, the combined budget for the security agencies (Defense and Navy) was up to USD$5.5 billion. Both the Ministry of Defense and the Navy have taken an active role in the fight against drug traffickers and drug cartels, mainly cooperating with the Ministry of Public Security (SSP) and with other law enforcement agencies, such as the Office of Attorney General (PGR) and the Center of National Security and Intelligence (CISEN). These three entities also received significant resources in 2011 (USD $6.1 billion). At the same time, state and local government consumption is not as large as the federal, but it is relevant, considering that each state has its own public security budget.

Regarding the safety industry, safety standards are an integral part of any manufacturing operation. Although Mexico has not had a strong preventive culture, this is changing due to globalization, higher flows of direct foreign investment, increased awareness of productivity, and lowering operative costs. The presence of multinational OEM's are bringing to Mexico safety requirements observed in their global operations plants, and these large corporations demand that their supply chain partners maintain safety standards too. Mexican businesses are modifying their internal practices and realize the importance of acquiring safety equipment and products to increase the security of their assets. Recently, the Mexican Ministry of Labor required all companies to comply with the corresponding regulations to operate their factories.

Best Prospects/Services

Best prospects for products and services in the security and safety sector include:
Government:
- Access control solutions
- Perimeter surveillance
- Electronic devices for mobile phones
- Biometric solutions
- Tactical equipment
- Personal protection products
- Communications systems (wireless, internet, GPS, etc.)

- Integrated security solution (compatibility/integration services)
- High-tech night vision tactical equipment
- Infra-red cameras/equipment

Commercial
- CCTV
- Perimeter protection solutions
- Access control
- Alarms
- Digital system (analog systems are being displaced)

- Residential solutions
- Personal protection devices
- Industrial protection accessories (safety goggles and earplugs)
- Industrial protection suits and gloves
- Communication integration services
- Anti-static uniforms/apparel

Opportunities

The scope of security and safety products is diverse, but the consumption of personal protection products, alarms, CCTV, residential protection solutions, and even electronic security devices is expected to increasesignificantly in the commercial market. Government purchases continue to be large in body protection equipment, combat systems, CCTV, personal and transportation GPS (chip), security vehicles and maintenance services, as well as for military and defense equipment.

Smart Grid

Overview

Efforts to modernize Mexico's electrical grid began in earnest with the 2010 publication of the country's National Energy Strategy (NES), which laid the foundation and objectives to carry out the country's overall energy reform based on energy security, efficiency, and sustainability guidelines. Mexico's Ministry of Energy and its state-owned utility (CFE) envision the smart grid as an enabler of some of NES's key lines of action, which include reducing the percentage of electrical power loss from 2010 levels of 17.5% to internationally accepted standards of 8% and generating 35% of the country's electricity from clean sources by the year 2024.

Thus far, actions have been focused on the development of a plan and vision for the Mexican smart grid. Significant progress has been made through initiatives such as CFE's application of the U.S SoftwareEngineering Institute's Smart Grid Maturity Model and the Energy Regulatory Commission's membership in the Smart Grid Interoperability Panel founded by the U.S. National Institute of Standards and Technology (NIST). These are two examples of collaborations with international organizations that have been crucial to developing Mexico's smart grid vision and strategy.

Mexico's smart grid activities to date have included the implementation of strategic pilot programs used to evaluate new technologies for their technical, operating and cost-benefit soundness. The ultimate goal of these pilot project and other research and international collaboration efforts is to shape a Smart Grid Roadmap — currently being developed— that will set a single, integrated global timeline for CFE's smart grid deployment.

Market Challenges
One of the most important challenges to the development of the smart grid market in Mexico is the absence of a specific legal framework and smart grid mandate, which has contributed to a prevalence of isolated efforts and a lack of coordination. It should be noted, however, that in spite of this lack of legal backing, the Mexican Ministry of Energy, the Energy Regulatory Commission and CFE have had the institutional conviction to move forward with grid modernization and projects are now conceived and carried out in a more coordinated and strategic manner.

A second challenge lies in CFE's budgetary constraints. The company has a specific mandate to procure at the lowest possible cost, which creates difficulties in integrating new technologies into its congressionally approved annual budget. CFE must convince the Ministries of Finance (which regulates power fees) and Energy that new technologies will eventually be more cost effective and improve the quality of service to consumers. At this stage, CFE also needs to overcome organizational issues that hinder the consolidation of a coordinated, benchmark evaluation process.

Market Opportunities
Development of the Mexican smart grid marketis mostly driven by the country's energy efficiency and renewable energy goals, which include increase grid reliability and efficiency and integration of clean energy. Taking this into account along with the fact that modernization is at an early stage, opportunities lie in the promotion of technologies suitable for CFE pilot programs. The prevention of power loss is a first priority and SMI metering projects are currently being implemented in different cities, with a major installation of 26,000 smart meters in Mexico City currently in the pipeline.

Integration of clean energy is seen as a midterm objective. Although most of Mexico's clean generation is hydroelectric, the country is building up its wind energy capacity with an investment of US$2.5 billion and 600 Megawatts to be tendered this year. These initiatives have been complemented by legislative changes that have tempered CFE's lowest cost procurement mandate with provisions for the consideration of environmental externalities and cap removals on the integration of renewable energies into the national grid.

Although CFE has a complete monopoly on transmission and distribution, the firm is only responsible for 60% of Mexico's power generation. Since 1992, the market for generation has been open to heavily regulated but growing private sector participation. It is expected that deployment of smart grid technologies will substantially increase private power producers, thus bringing more secondary buyers into the market.

In addition, Mexico's proximity to and common border with the U.S. incites collaboration on policy, standards, interoperability, and security thus creating advantages for U.S. firms

Best Products/Services
Immediate opportunities lie in distribution, with efficiency and reliability as the primary concerns. Best products include metering hardware and communications software for data management.

Opportunities for energy storage and other technologies to integrate power from fluctuating or weather-dependent sources into the grid will increase in the mid-term (approximately 6 years), although isolated pilot projects may be put in place in the short term.

Market Entry Strategy
CFE's procurement process can be either by invitation or by open international tender. The company is open to new technologies and welcomes commercial presentations, which may lead to tender invitations or specific technology recommendations. U.S. companies can work with the U.S. Commercial Service to make initial contact with CFE. The U.S. Commercial Service can also provide assistance in identifying and reaching out to local potential joint-venture partners for U.S. firms. Foreign companies often form consortiums with Mexican vendors to compete in CFE tenders, benefitting from their partners' local expertise.

Telecommunications Equipment

Overview

	2009	2010 (est.)	2011 (est.)
Total Market Size	10,190	11,413	12,324
Total Local Production	6,977	7,815	8,439
Total Exports	4,061	4,549	4,912
Total Imports	7,274	8,147	8,797
Imports from the U.S.	4,374	4,899	5,290

In September 2010 Mexico registered 33 million people with Internet access; this represents a more than 20% growth compared to the same period in 2009. According to the telecom regulator, Cofetel, and the National Institute of Statistics and Geography (INEGI), 67% of Internet users are between 12 and 34 years old. Today Mexico shares a 50%-50% gender split between men and women that use PCs/Internet. Regarding online purchases, approximately 1.63 million people made a purchase or a payment online.

In the 2010 census, INEGI reported over 112 million people in Mexico and 25 million households. Today there are an estimated 6 million Internet connections, reaching approximately 25% of the population. Much of the growth in Internet penetration will be from Cable TV Triple Play Service, given that over 40% of households in Mexico have access to cable.

According to Iván Marchant, Country Manager for comScore México,"The outlook for Internet in Mexico continues to prosper as one of the fastest growing markets worldwide..." Today, the Microsoft portal has over 16.2 million users, while Google has over 15.2 million users, and with a 200% growth between 2009 and 2010, Facebook now reaches 11.6 million users.

Today, we can safely mention that Dial Up service is basically extinct in Mexico. All communications companies offer broadband Internet access and cost is differentiated by the capacity of broadband. The most common service is a 1Mb connection but 2 Mb is becoming standard. There are other residential packages that offer up to a 20 Mb connection.

All communications companies offer standard communications and Internet services. Fixed line companies like Telmex, Alestra, Axtel, and Maxcom seek to bundle Double or Triple Play services, but in the case of Maxcom, it offer Quadruple Play services. However, the biggest winners in the Triple Play offer have been Cable TV (CATV) fixed operators. They have grown in Pay-TV services and Internet connection subscribers. The biggest players in the CATV industry are Megacable, Cablemás, and Cablevisión. Additionally, wireless operators are compensating the slow voice growth with smartphones, data services, and applications. More and more people are trading in their cell phones for smartphones and other devices that have wireless connectivity, such as tablets, netbooks, and modems.

Best Products/Services and Opportunities
For U.S. companies seeking to enter Mexico through the offer of software, hardware, applications, or other products or services to operators, the main companies in the telecom market in Mexico are:

Wireless: Telcel, Movistar, Nextel, Iusacell / Unefon
Fixed: Telmex, Alestra, Axtel, Maxcom
Cable: TV Megacable, Cablemás, Cablevisión

For the above-mentioned carriers, their demand for services will grow in different areas such as:

- Business Intelligence Software
- CATV Network Applications
- Consulting & IT/Systems Integration
- Information Security Services
- Leased Infrastructure (NOCs, SOCs)
- Maintenance & Service
- Tailored Software Applications for Vertical Markets
- Training (bundled with an overall solution)
- Wireless Applications (mainly focused on mobile broadband, such as TV)

The Mexican user market is quickly moving to service contracts as the predominant business model. Software, Infrastructure and Platform as a Service (SaaS, IaaS, and PaaS) will provide the best opportunities. Also, the general technology trends are present in Mexico where new opportunities will arise. These are:

- Cloud Computing and network terminals using web-based applications
- Green IT equipment for Data Centers
- Mobile Broadband
- Online Advertising
- Social Networks
- Virtualization
- Web 2.0
- Wimax equipment, 3G and LTE (4G) equipment for mobile carriers

Opportunities

There are various opportunities in the telecom sector. Carriers are increasing their spectrum capacity and targeting 3G and LTE (4G) networks, where the main players are Telmex, Axtel, Alestra, Maxcom, América Móvil, Iusacell, Nextel, and Telefónica. The telecom equipment OEM's (Nokia-Siemens, NEC, Cisco, Ericsson, Huawei, Alcatel-Lucent, ZTE, and Juniper Networks) actively pursue these opportunities. However, inventory management of parts and 2nd tier equipment can fulfill carriers' specific requirements.

Also, cloud computing solutions, mobile applications, equipment maintenance, and services are good prospective opportunities for U.S. companies who wish to enter Mexico through a local strategic partner.

Finally, data center solutions (hardware,software, and services), including green solutions, will provide good opportunities in the next few years.

Transportation Infrastructure Equipment and Services

Overview

Figures in millions of US dollars:

	2010	2011 (est.)	2012 (est.)
Total Market Size	1,977	2,164	2,272

Total Local Production	4,023	4,120	4,320
Total Exports	3,433	3,604	3,812
Total Imports	1,120	1,260	1,325
Imports from the U.S.	735	806	846

The Mexican transportation sector is facing one of the most important challenges in its history. The huge increase in Mexican foreign trade, in addition to the increase in traffic of merchandise arriving at Mexican ports with final destinations to the U.S. and Canada, requires a quick response from the transportation sector to improve efficiency, cost savings and cargo security.

Although railroads have increased their participation in the transportation sector, they still have low participation in cargo movement in Mexico. Figures presented by the Secretaria de Comunicaciones y Transportes (Secretariat of Communications and Transportation) on July 31,2011, indicated that 584 million tons in goods were transported across Mexico with 61 percent of cargo moved by truck, 12 percent by railroad, and 27 percent through maritime ports. Currently, Mexico has 74 intermodal terminals operating, including 30 interior multimodal terminals, 18 railroad terminals, 18 port terminals, and eight private automotive terminals. The goal of President Calderon's team is to increase the volume of cargo using railroad transportation by at least 18-20 percent in 2012, and to build nine new interior cargo terminals, two new port terminals, one new private automotive terminal, and 10 new multimodal corridors.

Although most of these projects were severely affected by the economic crisis, now the gradual economic recovery is allowing the public and private sectors to continue with initial plans to develop important transportation infrastructure projects. The Federal Government just announced that from 2007 to 2010, there was an investment of $ 14.4 billion dollars in road construction and modernization projects, including $ 1.9 billion dollars invested by public-private joint ventures. In 2011, construction started on six roads with a total of 293 kilometers.

In the port sector, several important projects started in 2011, including the expansion of the Port of Veracruz, that will take about 15-20 years to be completed, and will require investments of over USD $1.2 billion. This includes the construction of new port facilities in the Vergara Bay, just next to the current port location. Also in 2011, the Port of Lazaro Cardenas granted a concession for the construction of a new container terminal; the Port of Guaymas opened public bids for the construction of a new terminal and facilities to handle mineral bulks; the Port of Mazatlan began modernization of its multipurpose use terminal; and a new concessioner start the construction of a second container terminal in the Port of Manzanillo. Many projects that were on standby during 2009-2010 will be retaken by private investors, including improving facilities and building new private multimodal terminals and distribution centers.

Some companies are trying to develop new logistics services for pharmaceutical and medical supply chains that need special conditions for transportation, warehousing and handling. This niche could represent important opportunities for U.S. companies that are already offering these services or offer products for this kind of specialized logistics service.
Additionally, most transportation entities are looking for the best technologies to improve their services, increase customer satisfaction, assure cargo security, and promote an efficient transportation system that supports Mexico's competitiveness in a global world economy. Even with the current economic crisis, these trends have resulted in an important demand for all kinds of equipment and services that can help increase the efficiency of the transportation and logistics sector in Mexico.

All these projects and economic trends will gradually result in the recovery of the domestic production and the importation of equipment for the transportation sector.

Best Products/Services

Domestic production comprises low-tech equipment (such as front loaders, non-sophisticated traffic control systems, open and closed freight cars, and rail track fixtures) and strong production of trucks and trailers, including international corporations such as Chrysler, Freightliner, Mercedes Benz, International, and Kenworth, that are producing mainly for exports. However, all high-capacity cranes, railroad and lifting equipment are imported. Under NAFTA, most equipment for intermodal transportation manufactured in the U.S. can be imported duty free.

Products having the best prospects in this market include: frame, mobile and rotary cranes, self-propelled cranes on tires, front loaders with a capacity of over 7 tons, mobile platforms, traffic- control equipment, diesel electric locomotives, railway maintenance service vehicles, rail and tramway freight cars, automatic unloading wagons, covered and closed cars, assemblies for railway vehicles, containers, chassis, and trailers.

Opportunities

From January to October 2010, the U.S. supplied 61 percent of the sector's total imports, a six percent increase over the 2009 market share of 55 percent of the import market. This share could be increased if American firms take full advantage of NAFTA conditions and become more aggressive in the sector. The U.S. Commercial Service can provide information on new projects and support introduction of products into this market.

Travel and Tourism Services

Overview

Mexican Arrivals to the U.S. (in millions of travelers):

	2010	2011 (est.)	2012 (forecast)
Total Arrivals from Mexico	13.47	13.60	14.15
Percent Change	2%	1%	4%
Total Air Arrivals	1.67	1.68	1.75
Percent Change	11%	1%	4%

The United States is the most important destination for Mexican travelers. In 2010, 13.47 million Mexicans traveled to the United States, representing almost a quarter of the total foreign arrivals to the country. In 2010, Mexico was the second source of international travelers to the United States just after Canada. In 2010, Mexico reversed 2008 and 2009 declines which were a result of the adverse global economic environment. There was an increase of one percent during 2011 and four percent growth is expected in 2012.

In 2010 spending by Mexican travelers totaled $8.7 billion. Approximately 75% of this total is tied to the 1.67 million (12% of total number of visitors) Mexicans who traveled to the United States via air. U.S. travel and tourism companies are advised to consider this when preparing marketing strategies and promotional packages to potential Mexican tourists.

Best Products/Services

It is important to differentiate between land and air Mexican travelers to the United States. Mexican land tourists usually travel to the southern states for a short time period in order to visit relatives or friends and to shop. In contrast, air travelers usually stay longer and buy packages that include transportation, lodging, shopping, and recreational activities. These tourists are particularly lucrative since they are the ones who generate most of the travel and tourism receipts to the United States.

The Pacific and the Atlantic regions maintained the largest market shares for Mexican travelers to the United States. The top destinations, that are not strictly border visits, are California, Texas, Florida and New York in addition to Nevada, New Mexico, Colorado, Illinois and Georgia.

Opportunities

Mexicans are drawn to the United States because of its destination diversity, infrastructure, and excellent travel and tourism services. In particular, Mexicans enjoy destinations that offer shopping, gaming, entertainment, amusement parks, and a cosmopolitan environment. Natural parks and other outdoor destinations are typically not popular among Mexicans with skiing the notable exception – Mexicans flock to resorts in Colorado, New Mexico, and Utah in the winter months to ski.

Wholesale operators in Mexico continue to be an important distribution channel in the Mexican travel and tourism market. Wholesalers sell their packages to travel agents who provide their services to the end consumers. Mexicans prefer to buy vacation packages through a travel agency, though purchasing airfare and hotel packages online is slowly becoming more common. U.S. wholesalers and tour operators are key players in the Mexican market because they negotiate directly with U.S. travel and tourism service companies and are able to offer better prices and packages. Wholesalers in Mexico are now buying products and services from receptive tour operators in the United States to save money and facilitate processes.

However, the younger population in Mexico is becoming more attracted to buy travel packages on the internet. There are a few Mexican and Latin American companies that sell hotel rooms, air tickets, and travel packages through their own websites and offer good deals to the end consumer. Travelers have the option to pay for their travel to the United States by debit or credit card in fixed installments with no interest.

It is crucial to establish and maintain a personal relationship with the travel and tourism companies in Mexico. U.S. travel and tourism companies are advised to travel to Mexico and develop a comprehensive follow-up strategy to obtain sufficient exposure in the Mexican market and increase sales. Distributing promotional material at one trade show is not likely to generate meaningful results.

Agricultural Sector

<u>Overview</u>

With a growing population, an expanding economy and an increasingly market-oriented agricultural sector, Mexico remained the United States' third largest agricultural trading partner in 2011 accounting for nearly 12% of total U.S. agricultural exports. The United States remains Mexico's principal agricultural trading partner receiving almost 80% of Mexico's total exports. Specifically, Mexico exported a record $16.5 billion worth of agricultural products to the United States in 2011. Mexican demand for U.S. agricultural products increased 25% in 2011 with total U.S. exports valued at a record $18.9 billion. The U.S. overall market share is not likely to change as the geographic and tariff advantages that are enjoyed in Mexico are likely to continue to make the United States the best import option for most major agricultural goods. U.S. agricultural exports should increase even further in 2012 now that Mexico's imposition of punitive tariffs (applied after the U.S. Government suspended the U.S.-Mexico Cross-Border Trucking Demonstration Project) has been completed removed.

Since NAFTA was implemented in 1994, bilateral agricultural trade between the United States and Mexico has expanded dramatically. Mexico's agricultural exports to the United States have seen, on average, double-digit growth rates per year – growth rates twice as large as before NAFTA. At the same time, U.S. agricultural exports to Mexico have grown at similar rates, reflecting the mutually beneficial outcomes NAFTA has provided to both countries agricultural sectors.

The United States' major agricultural exports to Mexico in 2011 were (in billion U.S. dollars): coarse grains (3.3), red meats (1.9), soybeans (1.7), dairy products (1.2), wheat (1.0), poultry meat (0.85), cotton (0.78), sugar & sweeteners (0.72), feeds & fodder (0.60), soybean meal

(.59), processed fruits and vegetables (0.53), and feeds and animal fats (0.53).

The following tables summarize the market situation of commonly exported U.S. agricultural products to Mexico:

Mexico: Dairy Products (in 1000 Metric Tons)

	2010	2011	2012
Total Market Size	12,018	12,019	12,020
Total Local Production	11,655	11,678	11,679
Total Exports	22	24	24
Total Imports	353	341	341

Steady growth in dairy (fluid milk, cheese, butter, non-fat dry milk, and dry whole-milk powder) for 2010 through 2012 suggests the economy is recovering, but not as quickly as some members of the Mexican dairy industry would like to witness. Consumer purchasing power continues growing and an increasing number of consumers are capable of paying for high-value food items. In addition, the elimination of retaliatory tariffs on U.S. products due to the resolution of the U.S.-Mexico Cross-Border Trucking Demonstration Project should make some dairy products more affordable to a number of Mexican consumers.Finally, Mexican producers have been hurt by high feed costs, which, presents strong opportunities for U.S. dairy product suppliers.

Mexico: Meat (Beef and Pork) (in 1000 Metric Tons CWE)

	2010	2011	2012
Total Market Size	3,899	3,910	3,945
Total Local Production	2,916	3,000	3,025
Total Exports	181	295	310
Total Imports	983	910	920

Mexican red meat consumption is forecast to increase in 2012 as the economy and consumers' purchasing power continue recovering. Although total pork consumption is greater than beef consumption, pork consumption will increase at a rate lower than that of beef, mostly due to higher prices and the substitution by consumers away from pork towards poultry because it's perceived as a cheaper and "healthier" protein. In addition, Mexican meat processors will continue to use imported U.S. pork variety meats as well as bone-in cuts because domestic production is not sufficient to meet their demands. Furthermore, U.S. beef exports to Mexico will continue to increase as the Mexican economy recovers and the elimination of retaliatory duties on imported U.S. beef provides additional opportunities.

Mexico: Poultry Meat (Chicken & Turkey) (in 1000 Metric Tons)

	2010	2011	2012
Total Market Size	3,523	3,682	3,691
Total Local Production	2,821	2,932	2,902
Total Exports			
Total Imports	702	250	789

The United States continues to be the largest supplier of poultry products to Mexico. The top three products imported by Mexico are fresh/chilled mechanically deboned chicken meat, fresh/chilled turkey parts, and frozen chicken leg quarters (although imports of poultry products are increasingly diversified). As of February 13, 2012, Mexico was still carrying out an anti-dumping investigation into U.S. exports of chicken leg quarters which could limit growth of this protein export to Mexico. Most of Mexico's poultry meat imports are used in food manufacturing. The typical Mexican consumer continues to enjoy chicken, turkey, and egg products at competitive prices.

Mexico: Soybeans (in 1000 Metric Tons)

	2009/10	2010/11	2011/12
Total Market Size	3,680	3,711	3,751
Total Local Production	121	168	172
Total Exports	0	0	0
Total Imports	3,523	3,498	3,500
Imports from the U.S.	3,354	3,337	3,300

Domestic soybean consumption is expected to increase slightly by 25,000 MT in MY 2011/12 to 3.685 million MT, as a result of the moderate increases in feed demand. U.S.

soybean exports to Mexico are expected to remain practically unchanged in 2011/12 due to the moderate demand from the domestic poultry sector, which continues to be the major consumer of soybean meal in Mexico. This sector has been adversely impacted by high grain prices caused by the worst drought in over half a century coupled with a cold snap in late 2011 that has devastated cropland in nearly half of Mexico. According to industry sources, it is estimated that feed represents between 75-80 percent of the total cost of broiler production.

Soybean oil production in 2011/12 is expected to increase slightly (1.5 percent). Relatively stronger demand in the cooking oil and the hotel, restaurant, and institutional (HRI) sector is driving demand. Moreover, these sources expect that demand from the hotel and institutional sectors could continue growing in the medium term. Moreover, these sources have indicated that with slightly higher disposable incomes, the Mexican market could witness relatively bullish demand for vegetable oils in 2011/12 (mainly in the cooking oil sector).

Mexico: Fresh Fruits (Apples, Pears, Grapes) (in 1000 Metric Tons)

	2009/10	2010/11	2011/12
Total Market Size	1,118	1,173	1,205
Total Local Production	779	824	840
Total Exports	128	171	150
Total Imports	339	349	365
Imports from the U.S.	305	306	331

The United States is the largest supplier of apples, pears, and grapes to the Mexican market and this trend should continue. Apple import levels depend heavily on the peso/dollar exchange rate, but the U.S. apple industry has successfully marketed U.S. apples through in-store promotions to retain their dominant market position. The domestic supply of pears is supplied by imports, primarily from the United States, and wholesale markets remain the most important fruit distribution channel for U.S. pears. Mexico is an important market for both U.S. and Chilean grapes. Promotional efforts have increased consumption, creating space for increased imports (70% U.S. origin) and increased domestic production. Resolution of the U.S.-Mexico Cross-Border Trucking Dispute led to the elimination of retaliatory tariffs and is expected to result in increased imports of U.S. apples, pears and grapes.

Best Products/Services
In 2011, Mexico imported almost $19 billion worth of U.S. agricultural, fishery, and forestry products – an increase of 25% from the previous year. Exports are expected to increase even higher in 2012 now that Mexico's imposition of punitive tariffs (applied after the U.S. Government suspended the U.S.-Mexico Cross-Border Trucking Demonstration Project) has been completed eliminated. The increase in U.S. exports to Mexico in 2011 has occurred across many product categories, such as coarse grains; red meats; soybeans and products including meal and oil; dairy products; wheat; poultry meat; cotton; sugar and sweeteners; feeds and fodder; processed fruits and vegetables; animal fats; fresh fruit; snack foods; and rice.

Demand for organic food products in Mexico has been growing over the last few years along with the overall trend of healthier eating. Organic foods are perceived by many Mexican consumers to be healthier than conventional foods. Mexico is now considered the second most obese country in the world and the Mexican government has made it a priority to reverse this through education campaigns and new food nutrition laws targeting school children. As a result, a growing number of Mexican consumers are pursuing healthier lifestyles which include better eating habits. This makes Mexico an attractive market for U.S. exporters of organic and other healthy food products.

A wine culture is developing in Mexico making this an attractive market for U.S. wine exporters. Market analysts estimate an annual 12% growth rate in consumption in the next few years. Mexico's transition to more wine consumption over other alcoholic beverages, increased interest among different consumer sectors including women and young adults, and growing interest among consumers in trying novel wines makes Mexico an excellent market for the promotion and sales of U.S. wines

Chapter 5: Trade Regulations and Standards

Import Tarriffs

Under the terms of the NAFTA, Mexico eliminated tariffs on all remaining industrial and most agricultural products imported from the United States on January 1, 2003. The remaining tariffs and non-tariff restrictions on corn, sugar, milk powder, orange juice, and dried beans were phased out as of January 1, 2008.

Duties assessed related to the cross-border trucking dispute were removed October 21, 2011 as a new cross-border trucking program was established.

A few U.S. exports are subject to antidumping duties that limit access to the Mexican market. A list of these products can be found at:
http://ia.ita.doc.gov/trcs/foreignadcvd/mexico.html

To prevent potential dumping practices, the Mexican authorities have set minimum prices for a wide range of imported products, including textiles, clothing, leather products, shoes, some metals, stationary products, tools, some glass products, bicycles, children's accessories, and others. These minimum prices will be taken as the base for calculating any duty or tax, if applicable, for all products imported under certain Harmonized System Codes.

Mexico has also implemented what are called "Sectoral Promotion Programs (PROSEC)" which reduce MFN tariffs to 0 or 5 percent on a wide range of important inputs needed by Mexico's export manufacturing sector. This program includes some 20 different industry sectors and affects 16,000 tariff line items. Mexican companies must be registered under this program to participate. It can be difficult to qualify.

All NAFTA-compliant products imported definitively into Mexico no longer need to pay the customs processing fee (CPF). Products temporarily imported for processing and re-export may be subject to the CPF since the imports are not considered "definitive."

The import duty, if applicable, is calculated on the U.S. plant value (f.o.b. price) of the product, plus the inland U.S. freight charges to the border and any other costs listed separately on the invoice and paid by the importer. These can include charges such as export packaging, inland freight cost, and insurance.

In addition, Mexico has a value-added tax (IVA) on most sales transactions, including sales of foreign products. The IVA is 11 percent for products staying in the Mexican border region, within twenty miles of the border, and 16 percent for products that enter the interior of Mexico. Basic products such as food and drugs (but not processed foods) are exempt from the IVA.

A special tax on production and services (IEPS) is assessed to the importation of alcoholic beverages, cigarettes and cigars, among others. This tax may vary from 25 to 160 percent depending on the product.

Where an "arms length" transaction does not exist between seller and importer, such as intra-company sales or transfers, Mexico applies valuation rules that are compatible with the Brussels Customs Valuation Code. Goods for which the NAFTA preferential tariff treatment is not requested are valued on a C.I.F. basis.

Trade Barriers

Under the NAFTA, there are virtually no tariff barriers for U.S. exports to Mexico, with the exception as noted above.

U.S. companies do, however, face certain non-tariff barriers when exporting to Mexico. In November 1992, Mexico published a list of goods (with several subsequent updates and expansions) previously susceptible to fraudulent customs under-valuation and established a "minimum estimated price" for such goods.

Minimum estimated prices, also referred to as a "reference price", no longer affect goods other than used cars, as per resolution published in the Diario Oficial on January 26, 2009.

New requirements include a Vehicle Identification Number (VIN, or NIV) confirming that the vehicle was manufactured in the United States, Mexico or Canada; compliance with standard vehicle categories; and the payments of IVA (value added tax), ISAN (vehicle's acquisition tax), as well as a 10% ad-valorem tax (3% for border zone*) based on reference pricing established for the given year, make, and model of the vehicle.

Used vehicles destined for the border zone are only permitted if less than 10 years old and those older than 5 years but less than 10 years are mandated to remain in that zone. Used vehicles aged eight to ten years are permitted in the rest of Mexico for resale. In 2013 this will be expanded to cars aged 6-10 years old. Used vehicles of a condition which are restricted or prohibited from circulating in their own country of origin, are prohibited from importation into Mexico.

Please refer to the market report on regulations for the importation of used vehicles and trucks into Mexico for further details.
http://www.buyusainfo.net/docs/x_3353354.pdf

Certain sensitive products must obtain an import license for which the difficulty varies according to the nature of the product. Periodically, the Mexican government publishes lists that identify the different items that have a specific import control. Items are identified according to their Harmonized System (HS) code number; therefore, it is important that U.S. exporters have their products correctly classified. U.S. exporters are encouraged to check with customs brokers as to the accurate classification of their products.

The following are examples of import licenses required and the Mexican government agencies that administer the particular licenses. Note that this is not a complete list.

- The Secretariat of Economy requires import licenses for weapons and ammunition, used goods, and refurbished equipment, among others.
- The Secretariat of Agriculture (SAGARPA) requires prior import authorization for some leather and fur products, fresh/chilled and frozen meat, and agricultural machinery among others.
- The Secretariat of Health (SSA) requires either an "advance sanitary import authorization" or "notification of sanitary import" for medical products and equipment, pharmaceuticals, diagnostic products, toiletries, processed food, and certain chemicals. Food supplements and herbal products are highly regulated in Mexico, unlike in the United States. In some cases only pharmaceutical-like companies may be eligible to import them.
- The Secretariat of the Environment (SEMARNAT) requires import authorizations for products made from

endangered species such as eggs, ivory, certain types of wood, furs, etc.

•Toxic and hazardous products have to comply with import authorization from an interagency commission called CICOPLAFEST which has representation from the four agencies mentioned above. This list includes a large number of organic and inorganic chemicals.

Commercial samples of controlled products shipped by courier are also subject to these regulations. As of June 2008, liquid, gas, and powdered products are no longer eligible to be shipped by courier, even in small quantities. Instead, these products must be shipped as a regular full-scale shipment would, with the use of a customs broker. Some special treatment may apply in the case of samples intended for research, product registration or certification. Unless returned at the sender's expense, Customs often confiscates or destroys samples lacking the proper documentation.

Import Requirements and Documentation

For tax purposes, all Mexican importers must apply and be listed on the "Padrón de Importadores" maintained by the Secretariat of Finance and Public Credit (Hacienda). In addition, Hacienda maintains special sector registries. To be eligible to import more than 400 different items, including agricultural products, textiles, chemicals, electronics, and auto parts, Mexican importers must apply to Hacienda to be listed on these special industry sector registries. Infrequently, U.S. exporters have encountered problems when products are added to the list without notice or importers are summarily dropped from the registry without prior notice or subsequent explanation.

The basic Mexican import document is the "pedimento de importación." This document must be accompanied by a commercial invoice (in Spanish), a bill of lading, documents demonstrating guarantee of payment of additional duties for undervalued goods (see "Customs Valuation") if applicable, and documents demonstrating compliance with Mexican product safety and performance regulations (see "Standards"), if applicable. The import documentation may be prepared and submitted by a licensed Mexican customs house broker or by an importer with sufficient experience in completing the documents.

Products qualifying as North American must use the NAFTA Certificate of Origin in order to receive preferential treatment. This must be completed by the exporter and does not have to be validated or formalized.

Unless the importer is accredited to act as a Mexican customs broker, the participation of a professional customs broker is necessary to ensure compliance with Mexico's customs regulations. Mexican customs law is very strict regarding proper submission and preparation of customs documentation. Errors in paperwork can result in fines and even confiscation of merchandise as contraband. Exporters are advised to ensure that Mexican clients employ competent, reputable Mexican importers or customs house brokers. Because customs brokers are subject to sanctions if they violate customs laws, some have been very restrictive in their interpretation of Mexican regulations and standards.

U.S. Export Controls

Mexico is not subject to any special U.S. export control regulations, and is designated as a Category I country (the least restrictive) for receipt of U.S. high technology products.

Temporary Entry

Temporary imports for manufacturing, transformation, and repair, under the IMMEX (Industria Maquiladora para Exportacion Maquila) program, are subject to payment of duties, taxes and compensatory fees. Other temporary imports from the United States, however, do not pay import duties, taxes orcompensatory fees, but they must comply with all other obligations set forth in Article 104 of the Mexican Customs Law. There are different types of temporary imports into Mexico, including:

a) Temporary imports to be returned in the same condition;
b) Instruments of foreign artists;
c) Temporary imports for cultural and sporting events;
d) Temporary imports for conventions, congresses and trade shows; and
e) Temporary imports for the press, journalism, and cinematography.

The procedures for category (a) are as follows: Category (a) applies to temporary imports that remain in Mexico for a limited time and with a specific purpose and are returned to the United States in the same condition and within the time limits established in the Law (Art. 106). Such is the case of demonstration equipment that is temporarily imported into Mexico for exhibitions or sales visits. In such cases, U.S. representatives do not need to contract the services of a Mexican customs broker, and may themselves do the declaration of the products to Mexican Customs, using the declaration lane at the time of entry. Overlooking this requirement may result in the confiscation of the products without possibility of recovery, unless a high penalty fee is paid to the Mexican Government. Temporary imports may remain in Mexico for up to six months.

In the case of medical devices, interested parties need to request an import permit for the specific show. The request needs to be submitted by a Mexican company authorized to sell/distribute medical devices in Mexico.

The import is processed under a temporary importation form and there are basic requirements to obtain the clearance from Customs, including:

1. A list of the products for temporary importation into Mexico;
2. A letter from the U.S. company stating that the product(s) is for temporary entry into Mexico and that it will not be sold;
3. A letter from the Mexican partner or company indicating that they take full responsibility for ensuring that the products are returned to the United States within the period allowed. The letter should also indicate that there is a business relationship between the Mexican party and the importer;
4. Preparation of a Temporary Customs Entry form (Pedimento de Importación Temporal);
5. The list of the products to be temporarily imported into Mexico must also be presented to U.S. Customs before the equipment enters Mexico in order to facilitate the duty free return to the United States.

For temporary imports related to the manufacture, transformation, or repair under the IMMEX program, exporters should obtain expert advice from a Mexican customs broker or other consultant with expertise in this area. More detailed information on this and the other categories of temporary imports may be obtained by contacting Manuel Velazquez of the U.S. Commercial Service Mexico Monterrey office. (Manuel.velazquez@trade.gov.)

Effective May 2011 Mexico joined the ATA Carnet program enabling temporary import to Mexico through this program. More information about this program is available in Chapter 8.

Labeling and Marking Requirements

All products intended for retail sale in Mexico must bear a label in Spanish prior to their importation to Mexico. Products that must comply with commercial and commercial/sanitary information NOM's must follow the guidelines as specified in the applicable NOM.

For more detailed information see the "Labeling and Marking" in the Standards section below.

Prohibited and Restricted Imports

There are very few prohibited items in Mexico. A list of these items can be found at:
http://www.aduanas.sat.gob.mx/aduana_mexico/2008/pasaj eros/139_16781.html

In the case of medical devices and health care products, in addition to complying with applicable standards, foreign manufactured products need to have a legally appointed representative/distributor in Mexico and be registered with the Secretariat of Health (SSA), prior to being sold in Mexico. With the exception of blood, blood derivate products and organs, almost all medical products can be imported into Mexico, if they comply with the regulations.

Customs Regulations and Contact Information
U.S. exporters continue to be concerned about Mexican customs administration procedures, including insufficient prior notification of procedural changes, inconsistent interpretation of regulatory requirements at different border posts, and uneven enforcement of Mexican standards and labeling rules. Complaints have been increasing recently for certain products, in spite of the fact that Mexican Customs has been putting procedures in place to address issues of non-uniformity at border ports of entry. Agricultural exporters note that Mexican inspection and clearance procedures for some agricultural goods are long, burdensome, non-transparent and unreliable. Customs procedures for express packages continue to be burdensome, though Mexico has raised the de minimus level to fifty dollars from one dollar. However, Mexican regulation still holds the courier 100 percent liable for the contents of shipments.

Standards

Overview

The Secretaria de Economia, through the Mexican Bureau of Standards (DGN - Dirección General de Normas), is the organization with the authority to manage and to coordinate the standardization activities in Mexico. Its authority is derived from the Ley Federal de Metrología y Normalización(LFMN), enacted in 1988 to provide greater transparency and access by the public and interested parties to the standards development process. The implementing regulations (Reglamento de la Ley Federal sobre Metrología y Normalización) were published in Mexico's Official Gazette (DOF - Diario Oficial de la Federacion). In accordance with the Federal Law, the Law of Metrology and Standardization and its Regulation (Reglamento de la Ley Federal sobre Metrología y Normalización), the National Program of Standardization (PNN - Programa Nacional de Normalización) is published annually in the DOF, which is the official document used to plan, inform and coordinate the standardization activities, both public and private, carried out by the Mexican Government.

Finally, two definitions are important to keep in mind:

1. NOMs – literally: Mexican Official Standards – these are Technical Regulations, including labeling requirements, issued by government agencies and ministries. Compliance is mandatory.

2. NMX – Mexican "Voluntary" Standards – these are voluntary standards issued by recognized national standards-making bodies. Compliance is mandatory only when a claim is made that a product meets the NMX, when a NOM specifies compliance, and whenever applicable in government procurement.

Standards Organizations

The Mexican government entities that develop NOMs – Technical Regulations include:

- ECONOMIA (Commerce)
- SAGARPA (Agriculture)
- STPS (Labor)
- SCT (Communications & Transportation)
- SECTUR (Tourism)
- SEDESOL (Social Development)
- SEMARNAT (Environment)
- SENER (Energy)
- SSA (Health)

The DGN publishes the National Standardization Plan (PNN – Plan Nacional de Normalización) twice a year. It is available on the DGN website. Contact information is listed at the end of this chapter.

Organizations that develop NMX – Mexican "Voluntary" Standards include:

- ANCE (Electrical)
- IMNC (Quality Systems)
- INNTEX (Textiles)
- ONNCCE (Construction)
- NORMEX (Food Products and Quality Systems)
- NYCE (Electronics)

NIST Notify U.S. Service:

Member countries of the World Trade Organization (WTO) are required under the Agreement on Technical Barriers to Trade (TBT Agreement) to report to the WTO all proposed technical regulations that could affect trade with other Member countries. Notify U.S.is a free, web-based e-mail subscription service that offers an opportunity to review and comment on proposed foreign technical regulations that can affect your access to international markets. Register online at Internet URL: http://www.nist.gov/notifyus/

Conformity Assessment

Under NAFTA, Mexico was required, starting January 1, 1998, to recognize conformity assessment bodies in the United States and Canada on terms no less favorable than those applied in Mexico. After years of negotiations, two U.S. certification bodies were finally accredited. More recently, on August 17, 2010, the Secretariat of Economy published in the Mexican Official Gazette an agreement and amendments to the foreign trade general regulations to unilaterally accept as equivalent product certifications from U.S. and Canadian certifying bodies. The three Mexican technical regulations included in this equivalency agreement are NOMs 001-SCFI (audio and video equipment), 016-SCFI (office electrical appliances) and 019-SCFI (information technology equipment-safety). This agreement is expected to facilitate U.S. exports to Mexico.

Currently, only certificates issued by the following three U.S. - based certifying bodies have been accepted as equivalent by the Mexican government:

1) Intertek Testing Services NA, Inc.
2) TÜV Rheinland of North America, Inc.
3) Underwriters Laboratories, Inc.

However, given the differences between US and Mexican conformity assessment systems, significant custom-import logistical challenges remain unresolved.

Based on agreements with other agencies, as well as with other certification organizations, the DGN has established procedures for the certification of products to both Technical Regulations (NOMs) and Voluntary Standards (NMXs).

Conformity Assessment procedures issued by the SE/DGN tend to be more fully developed and cover a significantly greater range of NOMs than those of other ministries that develop NOMs.

Product Certification

For the purposes of the certification procedure, the following definitions are issued:

Product Certification: Proof of compliance with the applicable Mexican standard. An accredited certification body must issue these certificates.

DGN: General Bureau of Standards, Ministry of Economy (SE). This agency authorizes the operation of certification and calibration laboratories and verification units, according to the Federal Law of Standardization and Metrology.

Accredited Laboratory: Institutions authorized to test or calibrate products subject to Mexican standards.

Accredited Unit for Sampling Verification: Third-party authorized inspection and product sampling.

NOM: Technical Regulation (mandatory)

NMX: Mexican Standard (voluntary)

Product Certification Organization: Product Certification Organization accredited by DGN through EMA (Entidad Mexicana de Acreditación – Mexican Accreditation Agency)

Quality System Certification Organization: Organization accredited by DGN through EMA to certify Quality Assurance Systems.

MRAs (mutual recognition agreements)

There is a significant number of MRAs (mutual recognition agreements) between Mexican and U.S. organizations. However, at present, none of these agreements exempt U.S. products from complying with all applicable Mexican technical regulations and product certification requirements. MRAs are mainly to recognize testing procedures. U.S.

exporters should check with the appropriate Mexican certification body as to the existence of any MRAs.

Accreditation

In 1999, the Mexican government authorized the first private organization to accredit conformity assessment bodies (calibration laboratories, certification bodies, testing laboratories, and verification/inspection units). This private non-profit institution is known as EMA (Entidad Mexicana de Acreditación - Mexican Accreditation Entity).

Calibration Laboratories:
Calibration laboratories are responsible for transferring the precision of reference standards to the measurement instruments used in the commercial and industrial sectors. The calibration laboratories can be sponsored by public or private organizations, including universities, professional associations and private companies. Individuals interested in performing calibration activities can obtain certification after meeting the certification requirements set by law.

Committees, made up of technicians and specialists in metrology, evaluate applications for certification as calibration laboratories. These committees make recommendations to the DGN for final decisions on certification. The committees also establish the technical specifications for the evaluation of calibration laboratories, set the precision requirements for the calibration chains and set the methods for comparison of standards.

Certification Bodies:
EMA has accredited several organizations for certifying compliance in different fields. The accreditation list includes but it is not limited to the following organizations:

ANCE –
Asociación de Normalización y Certificación (product certification body for the electric sector NOMs)

CALMECAC - Calidad Mexicana Certificada, A.C. (Certified Mexican Quality).

CNCP - Centro Nacional Para la Calidad del Plástico (Mexican Center for the Quality of Plastic).

CRT - Consejo Regulador Del Tequila (Tequila Regulation Council)

IMNC - Instituto Mexicano De Normalización y Certificación, A.C.(Mexican Institute of Standardization and Certification).

INNTEX - Instituto Nacional De Normalización Textil, A.C.(Mexican Institute of Textile Standardization).

NORMEX - Sociedad Mexicana de Normalización y Certificación, S.C.(Mexican Society of Standardization and Certification).

NYCE - Normalización y Certificación Electrónica (Electronic Standardization and Certification).

ONNCCE - Organismo de Normalización y Certificación de la Construcción y Edificación (Building and Construction Standardization and Certification Body)

UL de Mexico - Underwriters Laboratories de Mexico, S.A. de C.V. (Product certification body for electric and electronic equipment)

Intertek (Product certification body for electric and electronic equipment)

On July 6, 2007, the Secretariat of Economy published foreign trade rules and general criteria in the DOF, which lists all products by tariff number that must comply with a NOM at the point of entry into Mexico. This document is constantly updated to reflect cancellations or changes in NOMs or the application of new ones.

Testing Laboratories:

Testing laboratories are responsible for certifying that products meet Mexican standards and are normally commercial entities that make a profit from the testing of samples. The DGN through EMA is responsible for granting authorizations to test laboratories after receiving the recommendations of the Testing Laboratory Evaluating Committees (Comités de Evaluación de Laboratorios de Pruebas).

Each committee oversees a group of evaluators who visit the testing laboratories, review their organization, capabilities, staffs, etc. Testing laboratories must fully comply with standard NMX-EC-17025-IMNC-2006/ISO 17025:2005, which sets the requirements testing laboratories must comply with. Once the evaluators have made their review, they submit a report to the committee. Then, the committee writes its recommendations to the DGN, which, in turn, informs the laboratory of the results. Those applicants not receiving authorization are permitted to make the necessary modifications to their facilities in order to comply with standard NMX-EC-17025-IMNC-2006/ISO 17025:2005. After the committee verifies that the laboratory meets the requirements, a second report is prepared for the DGN.

Authorizations as testing laboratories are valid for two years and can be renewed upon written request. Testing laboratories are required to maintain their technical capabilities and to make any modifications that the committee may set. Testing laboratories must notify the DGN of any change in equipment, location, and administration. Laboratories have the option to withdraw their certification.

Verification Units:

Verification or inspection units check and provide a report or proof of compliance corroborated either visually or by sampling, measuring, testing in laboratories, or examining documents. Labeling NOMs, for example, do not require products to obtain a certificate of compliance; however, verification units can determine whether or not a technical regulation has been correctly applied.

On June 18, 2001, the Mexican standard NMX-EC-17020-IMNC-2000 (equivalent to ISO/IEC 17020:1998) went into effect to make the accreditation process of verification units consistent with international standards.

Publication of Technical Regulations

Publication of Proposed Technical Regulations:
In accordance with the Regulation of the Federal Law of Metrology and Standardization (Reglamento de la Ley Federal sobre Metrología y Normalización, LFMN), the National Program of Standardization (Programa Nacional de Normalización, PNN) is the official document used to plan, inform and coordinate the standardization activities, both public and private, carried out by the Mexican government. The PNN is made up of a list of topics that will be developed into technical regulations (NOMs), Mexican Standards (NMX's), and Reference Standards (NRF's)--as well as an approximate working calendar for each respective topic. The program is equally composed of information from the National Consulting Standardization Committees (Comités Consultivos Nacionales de Normalización), which are responsible for the creation of NOMs; the Technical Committees of National Standardization (Comités Técnicos de Normalización Nacional) and the National Standardization Bodies (Organismos Nacionales de Normalización), both of which are responsible for the creation of NMXs; and 2 Standardization Committees (Comités de Normalización), responsible for the creation of NRF's - standards created by governmental entities for government procurement.

The PNN is annually developed by the Technical Secretariat of the National Standardization Commission, revised by the Technical Council of the aforementioned entity, and approved by the National Standardization

Commission (CNN, Comisión Nacional de Normalización) in its first meeting of every year.

The LFMN and its Regulation establish a time frame for each step of the NOM-making process (development, draft publication in the DOF, and publication of modified and definitive technical regulations and standards) and within the PNN framework. The accomplishment of these tasks is limited to the span of a year. The actual NOM-making period, however, is contingent upon various factors, including the complexity of the topic and the uncertain period between each step (i.e. publishing period in the DOF, draft response, comments, and final technical regulation and standard). Therefore, evaluations of the PNN indicate, more often than not, that the standardization process requires more than a year in order to adequately meet its objectives.

U.S. entities can participate in the process in several ways. They can:

•Review the PNN to learn about the proposed standards.
•Participate in the applicable technical working group (requires physical presence).
•Submit commentaries during the 60-day public consultation period.
•Solicit the making, modification, or cancellation of technical regulations and standards (NOM and NMX) to the appropriate government office or to a National Standardization Body.

Labeling and Marking

All products intended for retail sale in Mexico must bear a label in Spanish prior to their importation to Mexico. Products that must comply with commercial and commercial/sanitary information NOMs must follow the guidelines as specified in the applicable NOM. Most NOMs require commercial information to be affixed, adhered, sewn, or tagged onto the product, with at least the following information in Spanish:

- Name or business name and address of the importer,
- Name or business name of the exporter,
- Trademark or commercial name brand of the product,
- Net contents (as specified in NOM-030-SCFI-2006 DOF November 4, 2006),
- Use, handling, and care instructions for the product as required,
- Warnings or precautions on hazardous products.

This information must be attached to the product, packaging or container, depending on the product characteristics. This information must be affixed to products as prepared for retail sale. Listing this information on a container in which a good is packed for shipment will not satisfy the labeling requirement.

NOMs do not explicitly state that country of origin is required on the label prior to importation. However, Mexican fiscal regulations do require country of origin designation, and the U.S. Department of Commerce recommends that exporters include this information, in Spanish, on the labels they are preparing for goods destined for retail sale in the Mexican market. Including the importer's taxpayer number (commonly known as RFC) is also recommended.

The commercial and commercial-sanitary NOMs currently in force are:

NOM-003-SSA1-2006, Environmental health - Sanitary requirements with which paints, inks, varnishes, lacquers, and enamels must comply, published in the DOF on August 4, 2008.

NOM-004-SCFI-2006, Commercial Information - Labeling of textile products, garments and accessories, published in the DOF on June 21, 2006.

NOM-015-SCFI-2007, Commercial Information - Labeling of toys, published in the DOF on April 17, 2008.

NOM-020-SCFI-1997, Commercial Information - Labeling of leather and leather-like goods, shoes and accessories published in the DOF on April 27, 1998.

NOM-024-SCFI-1998, Commercial Information for packaging, instructions, and warranties of electric and electronic products and appliances, published in the DOF on January 15, 1999.

NOM-050-SCFI-2004, Commercial information- General labeling of products, published in the DOF on June 1, 2004.

NOM-051-SCFI/SSA1-2010, General labeling specifications for pre packed food products and non-alcoholic beverages, published in the DOF on April 5, 2010.

NOM-055-SCFI-1994, Commercial Information - Fire retardants or inhibitors - published in the DOF on December 8, 1994.

NOM-072-SSA1-1993, Labeling of medicines, published in the DOF on April 10, 2000.

NOM-084-SCFI-1994, Commercial Information - Commercial and sanitary information specifications for pre packed tuna and bonito food products, published in the DOF on September 22, 1995.

NOM-116-SCFI-1997, Automotive industry - Commercial information of lubricant oils for gasoline or diesel engines, published in the DOF on May 4, 1998

NOM-120-SCFI-1996, Commercial Information - Labeling of agricultural products - Grape, published in the DOF on November 22, 1996.

NOM-128-SCFI-1998, Commercial Information - Labeling of agricultural products - Avocado, published in the DOF on August 31, 1998.

NOM-129-SCFI-1998, Commercial Information - Labeling of agricultural products - Mango, published in the DOF on August 31, 1998.

NOM-137-SSA1-2008 Labeling of medical devices, published in the DOF on December 12, 2008.

NOM-139-SCFI-1999, Commercial Information - Labeling of vanilla extract, derivatives and substitutes, published in the DOF on March 22, 2000.

NOM-141-SSA1-1995, Goods and services - Labeling of pre packed perfumery and beauty products, published in the DOF on July 18, 1997.

NOM-142-SSA1-1995, Goods and services. Alcoholic beverages. Sanitary specifications. Sanitary and commercial labeling published in the DOF on July 9, 1997.

NOM-189-SSA1/SCFI-2002, Products and services. Labeling and packaging of household cleaning products, published in the DOF on December 2, 2002.

NOM-232-SSA1-2009, Pesticides - Packaging and labeling requirements for technical grade products and those for agricultural, forest, garden, industrial, and household use, published in the DOF on April 13, 2012

Contacts
The following is key contact information for the most relevant organizations in both the
public and private sectors. For additional organizations, please contact the post.

Mexican Public Sector:
SE-Secretaria de Economía (Secretariat of Economy)

DGN-Dirección General de Normas (Mexican Bureau of Standards)
URL: http://www.economia.gob.mx/?P=85

SEMARNAT- Secretaria de Medio Ambiente y Recursos Naturales(Secretariat of the Environment and Natural Resources)
URL: http://www.semarnat.gob.mx

SCT – Secretaria de Comunicaciones y Transportes (Secretariat of Communications and Transportation)
URL : http://www.sct.gob.mx

COFEPRIS (FDA's Mexican Counterpart)
URL: http://www.cofepris.gob.mx/wb/cfp/ingles

Mexican Private Sector:
ANCE – Asociación de Normalización y Certificación del Sector Eléctrico, A.C. (National Association for the Standards & Certification of the Electrical Sector)
URL: http://www.ance.org.mx

COMENOR - Consejo Mexicano de Normalización y Evaluación de la Conformidad, A.C. (Mexican Council of Standardization and Conformity Assessment)
URL: http://www.comenor.org.mx

NYCE – Normalización y Certificación Electrónica, A.C. (Electronic Standards & Certification)
URL: http://www.nyce.org.mx

INMC – Instituto Mexicano de Normalización y Certificación, A.C. (Mexican Standards & Certification Institute)
URL: http://www.imnc.org.mx

NORMEX – Sociedad Mexicana de Normalización y Certificación, S.C. (Mexican Standards & Certification Society)
URL: http://www.normex.com.mx

ONNCCE – Organismo Nacional de Normalización y
Certificación de la Construcción y Edificación, S.C.
(National Body for the Standardization and Certification of
Construction and Buildings)
URL: http://www.onncce.org.mx

INNTEX- Instituto Nacional de Normalización Textil, A.C.
(National Institute of Textile Standards)
URL: http://www.cniv.org.mx/inntex

Post Standards Contacts:
U.S. Embassy – U.S. Commercial Service

Everett Wakai, Standards Attaché
Tel: (011-52-55) 5140-2603
Fax (011-52-55) 5535-1139
E-mail: Everett.Wakai@trade.gov
Liverpool 31, Col. Juárez
06600 México, D.F.
URL: http://www.BuyUSA.gov/mexico
and http://www.export.gov

Jesus S. Gonzalez, Commercial Specialist
Tel: (011-52-55) 5140-2627
Fax: (011-52-55) 5535-1139
E-mail: Jesus.Gonzalez@trade.gov
Liverpool 31, Col. Juárez
06600 México, D.F.
URL: http://www.BuyUSA.gov/mexico
and http://www.export.gov

U.S. Embassy – U.S. Department of Agriculture
Garth Thorburn, Director, Agricultural Trade Office
Liverpool 31, Col. Juárez
06600 México, D.F.
Tel: (011- 52-55) 5140-2611
 Fax: (011-52-55) 5535-8357
E-mail: Garth.Thorburn@usda.gov
URL: http://www.mexico-usda.com

Trade Agreements

An important feature of the U.S.-Mexico bilateral relationship is the North American Free Trade Agreement (NAFTA), which created a free trade zone for Mexico, the United States, and Canada. Since the enactment of NAFTA in January 1994, U.S. exports to Mexico have grown exponentially, totaling almost $200 billion in 2011. U.S. exports to Mexico are greater than U.S. exports to the rest of Latin America combined, and also greater than U.S. exports to the BRIC countries (Brazil, Russia, India, and China) combined. The U.S. share of Mexico's trade has likewise increased with NAFTA, accounting for nearly 75 percent of Mexico's total trade.

NAFTA continues to boost trade between the three member countries and improve Mexico's overall economic standing. Since the enactment of NAFTA in January 1994, total trade between the United States and Mexico has grown 423 percent. In 2011, there was 460 billion dollars in two way trade, with more than 1.25 billion dollars of goods crossing the border each day.

Mexico has more free trade agreements (FTA's) than any other country in the world. Mexico has FTA's with 43 countries (officially), including the European Union, European Free Trade Area, Israel, and 10 countries in Latin America. The agreement with the European Union was modeled after NAFTA and provides EU goods with the same benefits as NAFTA. The significance of this for U.S. exporters is that many of our strongest international trade competitors enjoy duty free access to the Mexican market equivalent to that provided by NAFTA – or if they do not today, they might in the near future. Mexico's membership in the WTO, the APEC, the OECD, and its pursuit of bilateral investment treaties give further testimony to Mexico's commitment to economic liberalization.

Chapter 6: Investment Climate

Openness to Foreign Investment

Mexico is open to foreign direct investment (FDI) in most economic sectors and has consistently been one of the largest recipients of FDI among emerging markets. It currently ranks second in attracting FDI in Latin America. In recent years, Mexico has become increasingly aware of its perceived loss of competitiveness and productivity relative to other emerging economies. Nevertheless, Mexico's macroeconomic stability and its proximity to one of the largest markets in the world have attracted investors. Broader economic reforms, as well as the nurturing a more flexible labor market and more competition in key sectors, are still needed to make the country more competitive. As it approaches presidential elections in July 2012, Mexico will need to focus on political and economic reforms if it is to increase its competitiveness as an FDI destination.

Foreign investment in Mexico has largely been concentrated in the northern states close to the U.S. border where most maquiladoras are located, and in the Federal District (Mexico City) and surrounding states, where most headquarters are located. According to the Secretariat of the Economy, Mexico is currently the top destination for aerospace manufacturing investments in the world. The Yucatan peninsula, historically an area for tourism investment, has seen notable growth due to its ability to quickly send goods to ports in the United States. Financial services, automotive and electronics have received the largest amounts of FDI. Historically, the United States has been the main source of FDI in Mexico. In 2011, U.S. investors accounted for 55 percent of all FDI in Mexico. United States FDI was largely concentrated in the manufacturing (47 percent) and commercial (16 percent) sectors.

In June 2007, ProMexico was created, a federal entity charged with promoting Mexican exports around the world and attracting foreign direct investment to Mexico. Through ProMexico, federal and state government efforts, as well as related private sector activities, are coordinated with the goal of harmonizing programs, strategies and resources while supporting the globalization of Mexico's economy. ProMexico maintains an extensive network of offices abroad as well as a multi-lingual website (http://www.investinmexico.com.mx) which provides local information on establishing a corporation, rules of origin, labor issues, owning real estate, the maquiladora industry, and sectoral promotion plans. ProMexico coordinated Mexico's hosting of the 2010 World Conference of Trade Promotion Agencies in the Riviera Nayarit. The Embassy advises potential investors to contact ProMexico for detailed information on investing in Mexico. From January to September 2011, ProMexico attracted 70 investment projects from the United States, Japan and South Korea, in the energy, automotive and auto parts sectors, totaling $9.26 billion.

The Secretariat of the Economy also maintains a bilingual website (www.economia.gob.mx) offering an array of information, forms, links and transactions. Among other options, interested parties can download import/export permit applications, make online tax payments, and chat with online advisors who can answer specific investment and trade-related questions. State governments have also passed small business facilitation measures to make it easier to open businesses. The Mexican government is currently developing an International Trade Single Window to simplify import, export, and transit-related operations, increase efficiency, and reduce costs and time for international traders.

According to the most recent World Bank Study "Doing Business 2012", Mexico succeeded in reducing the number of average days to complete all paperwork required to start a business from 28 days to 9 days, as well as the number of business procedures from 8 to 6. Mexico moved up one position, from 53 to 52, scoring better than Brazil, India, China and Russia. More information on the ranking can be found at: http://www.doingbusiness.org/rankings.

The 1993 Foreign Investment Law is the basic statute governing foreign investment in Mexico. The law is consistent with the foreign investment chapter of NAFTA (the North American Free Trade Agreement). It provides national (i.e. non-discriminatory) treatment for most foreign investment, eliminates performance requirements for most foreign investment projects, and liberalizes criteria for automatic approval of foreign investment. The Foreign Investment Law identifies 704 activities, 656 of which are open for 100 percent FDI stakes. There are 20 activities in which foreigners may only invest 49 percent; 13 in which Foreign Investment National Commission approval is required for a 100percent stake; five reserved only for Mexican nationals; and 10 reserved for the government of Mexico. Below is a summary of activities subject to investment restrictions:

Sectors Reserved for the State in Whole or in Part:
A. Petroleum and other hydrocarbons;
B. Basic petrochemicals;
C. Telegraphic and radio telegraphic services;
D. Radioactive materials;
E. Electric power generation, transmission, and distribution;

F. Nuclear energy;
G. Coinage and printing of money;
H. Postal service;
I. Control, supervision and surveillance of ports of entry.

Sectors Reserved for Mexican Nationals:
A. Retail sales of gasoline and liquid petroleum gas;
B. Non-cable radio and television services;
C. Development Banks (law was modified in 2008);
D. Certain professional and technical services;
E. Domestic transportation for passengers, tourism and freight, except for messenger or package delivery services.

U.S. and Canadian investors generally receive national and most-favored-nation treatment in setting up operations or acquiring firms in Mexico. Exceptions exist for investments in which the Government of Mexico recorded its intent in NAFTA to restrict certain industries to Mexican nationals. U.S. and Canadian companies have the right under NAFTA to international arbitration and the right to transfer funds without restrictions. NAFTA also eliminated some barriers to investment in Mexico, such as trade balancing and domestic content requirements. Local governments must also accord national treatment to investors from NAFTA countries.

Mexico is also a party to several OECD agreements covering foreign investment, notably the Codes of Liberalization of Capital Movements and the National Treatment Instrument.

Approximately 95 percent of all foreign investment transactions do not require government approval. Foreign investments requiring applications and not exceeding USD 165 million are automatically approved, unless the proposed investment is in a sector subject to restrictions by the Mexican constitution and the Foreign Investment Law that reserve certain sectors for the state and Mexican nationals. The National Foreign Investment Commission under the Secretariat of Economy determines whether investments in restricted sectors may go forward, and has

45 working days to make a decision. Criteria for approval include employment and training considerations, technological contributions, and contributions to productivity and competitiveness. The Commission may reject applications to acquire Mexican companies for national security reasons. The Secretariat of Foreign Relations (SRE) must issue a permit for foreigners to establish or change the nature of Mexican companies.

Despite Mexico's relatively open economy, a number of key sectors in Mexico continue to be characterized by a high degree of market concentration. For example, telecommunications, electricity, television broadcasting, petroleum, beer, cement, and tortillas feature one or two or several dominant companies (some private, others public) with enough market power to restrict competition. The Mexican Congress passed some amendments to the law to strengthen the enforcement powers of the Federal Competition Commission (COFECO) in 2011, but COFECO remains weak relative to its OECD counterparts in terms of enforcement. COFECO Commissioner Eduardo Perez Motta and leading members of the Calderon Administration, including the President, have publicly committed to opening up the Mexican economy to greater competition. For more information on competition issues in Mexico please visit COFECO's bilingual website at: www.cfc.gob.mx.

Energy: The Mexican constitution reserves ownership of petroleum and other hydrocarbon reserves for the Mexican state. The energy reform package approved by the Mexican Congress in October 2008 did not address this prohibition, and oil and gas exploration and production efforts remain under the sole purview of Pemex, Mexico's petroleum parastatal. While Pemex had previously contracted with foreign companies to perform specific tasks such as drilling wells, platform construction or equipment maintenance on a fee-for-service basis, the 2008 reform allowed some private participation in exploration and production of oil fields through so-called "integrated contracts". In 2011, Pemex successfully completed its first bidding process for three integrated contracts for mature oil fields in Southwest

Mexico. Pemex announced that it would solicit bids in 2012 for additional mature and inactive fields in the north of Mexico, followed by bids within the next few years for Chicontepec and deep water projects. The constitution also states that most electricity service may only be supplied by one state-owned company, the Federal Electricity Commission (CFE).

There has been some opening to private capital. Private electric co-generation and private or municipal power projects for self-supply are now allowed; companies involved in self-supply from renewable energy sources are also permitted to generate power to be fed into CFE's grid at one location and take off the equivalent amount of power at different locations for a nominal "postage stamp" charge. Companies or households producing up to 15 kilowatts of energy are allowed to supply the excess to CFE's grid and receive credit for the energy produced. Private investors may build independent power projects, but all of their output must be sold to CFE in wholesale transactions. Private construction of generation for export is permitted, including generation from renewable sources of energy, particularly wind. In 1995, amendments to the Petroleum Law opened transportation, storage, marketing and distribution of natural gas imports and issued open access regulations for Pemex's natural gas transportation network. Retail distribution of Mexico's natural gas is open to private investment, as is the secondary petrochemical industry. Pemex and CFE are also making plans to construct billions of dollars in new natural gas pipelines and are putting together tenders for financing and construction of these pipelines. Since the government's announcement in August 2001 that national and foreign private firms will be able to import liquefied petroleum gas duty-free, LNG terminals in Tamaulipas state and Baja California have begun operations, and CFE is building a third in Manzanillo, on Mexico's Pacific Coast.

Finance Public Works Contracts (COPFs), formerly Multiple Service Contracts (MSCs) designed to comply with the country's constitution, are Mexico's most ambitious effort to attract private companies to stimulate natural gas production by developing non-associated natural gas fields. Under a COPF contract, private companies will be responsible for 100 percent of the financing of a contract and will be paid for the work performed and services rendered. However, the natural gas produced in a specific field remains the property of Pemex. Examples of work that contractors can perform include seismic processing and interpretation, geological modeling, fields engineering, production engineering, drilling, facility design and construction, facility and well maintenance, and natural gas transportation services. Some Mexican politicians still oppose COPFs as a violation of the Mexican constitution's ban on concessions. Some contracts have failed to attract any bids, demonstrating the limited success of COPFs.

Telecommunications: Mexico allows up to 49 percent FDI in companies that provide fixed telecommunications networks and services. A bill to completely open fixed telecommunications networks to foreign investors has been introduced in Congress, but the bill has been delayed several times due to a demand to include a "reciprocity clause" that would open the sector in partner countries to Mexican companies. This includes the Cable TV (CATV) industry, with one exception: companies can issue Neutral or "N" stocks up to 99 percent, which can be owned by a foreign company. In fact, one CATV company operates under this ownership scheme. There is no limit on FDI for companies providing cellular/wireless services. However, Telmex and Telcel (América Móvil) continue to reign as the dominant telecom fixed and wireless providers and wield significant influence over key regulatory and government decision makers. Mexico's dominant landline and wireless carriers are traded on the New York Stock Exchange.

Several large U.S. and international telecom companies are active in Mexico, partnering with Mexican companies or holding minority shares. Following a 2004 WTO ruling, international resellers are authorized to operate in Mexico and some companies are also looking to sell wholesale minutes to resellers. Telcel (technically independent, but majority owned by Telmex owner's Grupo Carso - Carso Global Telecom) still retains a great majority share (over 70 percent) of the cellular market. However, Spain's Telefonica Movistar, among others, continues to grow and challenge the status quo, deploying extensive mobile infrastructure to increase coverage across the country. Telmex continues to dominate the market in Long Distance (domestic and international), Internet access through DSL, and bundle services. The Convergence Accord, published in October 2006, allowed Telmex to offer broadcasting or TV services. However, the Federal Telecommunications Commission ruled that Telmex must first comply with interconnection, interoperability and number portability requirements before receiving permission to complete its triple-play offering. The accord has elicited strong concerns from the CATV industry, which fears that it will push CATV operators to consolidate. Under the accord, CATV operators (including TV duopolist Televisa's Cablevision) are allowed to independently offer Triple Play Service (VoIP-Telephony, Data-Internet and TV-Video), which might increase competition in the telephony market.

As in telecommunications, there are concerns that the two dominant television companies -- Televisa and TV Azteca, who share duopoly status in the sector -- continue to exercise influence over Mexican judicial, legislative and regulatory bodies to prevent competition. However, in August 2007 the Mexican Supreme Court ruled against the most blatant anti-competition measures of the April 2006 Radio and Television Law. Among other decisions, the Court ruled that it was unfair for broadcasting companies to keep and use at no cost analog spectrum freed from the digitalization process. The Supreme Court mandated that the Mexican Legislature draft a new media law based on its ruling. At present, U.S. firms remain unable to penetrate the Mexican television broadcast market, despite the fact that both Televisa and TV Azteca benefit from access to the U.S. market.

In 2010, the Mexican government completed the much-awaited spectrum auction of the 1.7 GHz and 1.9 GHz bands. However, a domestic wireless operator aggressively challenged the Mexican courts on the awarding of the GHz band to a U.S wireless operator. The barrage of lawsuits delayed the company's plan to expand its wireless services. However, at the end of 2011 both companies reached an out-of-court settlement.

At the January 10, 2011 NAFTA Free Trade Commission meeting, the term sheet for the Comision Interamericana de Telecomunicaciones (CITEL) mutual recognition agreement was initialed. The agreement established procedures for accepting test results from laboratories or testing facilities in the territory of another NAFTA country for use in the conformity assessment of telecommunications equipment. This allows a manufacturer to test a product only once and then have the test results accepted in other NAFTA countries.

Real Estate: Investment restrictions still prohibit foreigners from acquiring title to residential real estate in so-called "restricted zones" within 50 kilometers (approximately 30 miles) of the nation's coast and 100 kilometers (approximately 60 miles) of the borders. In all, the restricted zones total about 40 percent of Mexico's territory. Nevertheless, foreigners may acquire the effective use of residential property in the restricted zones through the establishment of a 50-year extendable trust (called a fideicomiso) arranged through a Mexican financial institution that acts as trustee.

Under a fideicomiso, the foreign investor obtains all rights of use of the property, including the right to develop, sell and transfer the property. Real estate investors should, however, be careful in performing due diligence to ensure that there are no other claimants to the property being purchased. Fideicomiso arrangements have led to legal challenges in some cases. U.S. issued title insurance is available in Mexico and a few major U.S. title insurers have begun operations here. Additionally, U.S. lending institutions have begun issuing mortgages to U.S. citizens purchasing real estate in Mexico.

Transportation: The Mexican government allows up to 49 percent foreign ownership of 50-year concessions to operate parts of the railroad system, renewable for a second 50-year period. The Mexican Foreign Investment Commission and COFECO must approve ownership above 49 percent. Consistent with NAFTA, foreign investors from the U.S. and Canada are now permitted to own up to 100 percent of local trucking and bus companies, however, several companies have encountered long wait times and legal tie-ups when trying to obtain permits.
CINTRA, the government holding company for the Mexican airline groups, Mexicana and Aeromexico, sold Grupo Mexicana to Grupo Posadas in December 2005. Grupo Aeromexico was sold to a consortium led by Citibank-owned Banamex in October 2007. In 2010, Mexicana filed for a bankruptcy process and suspended its flights. Grupo Posada was forced to sell the airline to a new group of investors, and although there have been several interested and potential investors, the airline and the government have been so far unable to close a deal. The emergence of low-cost domestic airlines such as Volaris and Interjet have increased competition and led to lower prices. However, foreign ownership of Mexican airlines remains capped at 25 percent and foreign ownership of airports is limited to 49 percent. Foreign express delivery service companies continue to complain that Mexican legislation unfairly favors Mexican companies by restricting the size of trucks international carriers are allowed to use.

Infrastructure: Mexican infrastructure investment, with certain previously noted exceptions, is open to foreign investment. The Mexican government has been actively seeking an increase in private involvement in infrastructure development in numerous sectors, including transport, communications, and environment. Improvement in the national infrastructure is seen as a key element to strengthening economic competitiveness and attracting investment to disadvantaged regions of the country. In July 2007, President Calderon presented the National Infrastructure Program 2007-2012. A key aspect of this program is to increase private investment through means of Service Lending Projects (public-private partnerships) and concessionary schemes. Unfortunately, the credit crunch in 2008-2009 and a lack of planning have delayed spending in infrastructure. In 2011, the Public-Private Associations Law was approved by the lower house of Congress; the law had been approved by the Senate in October 2010. The Public-Private Partnership Law allows the government to enter into infrastructure and service provision contracts with private companies for up to 40 years.

The law provides more legal certainty to private investors by equally distributing risks, facilitates access to bank loans, and harmonizes existing state public-partnership models under a single federal law. National and foreign investors alike will be allowed to participate in the bidding process, except in restricted sectors as set forth by the Foreign Direct Investment law. More information on the Public-Private law can be found at: www.infraestructura.gob.mx

Expropriation and Compensation

Under NAFTA, Mexico may not expropriate property, except for public purpose and on a non-discriminatory basis. Expropriations are governed by international law, and require rapid fair market value compensation, including accrued interest. Investors have the right to international arbitration for violations of this or any other rights included in the investment chapter of NAFTA.

There have been twelve arbitration cases, of which two are still pending, filed against Mexico by U.S. and Canadian investors who allege expropriation, and other violations of Mexico's NAFTA obligations. Details of the cases can be found at the Department of State Website, Office of the Legal Advisor (www.state.gov/s/l).

Dispute Settlement

Chapter Eleven of NAFTA contains provisions designed to protect cross-border investors and facilitate the settlement of investment disputes. For example, each NAFTA Party must accord investors from the other NAFTA Parties national treatment and may not expropriate investments of those investors except in accordance with international law.

Chapter Eleven permits an investor of one NAFTA Party to seek money damages for measures of one of the other NAFTA Parties that allegedly violate those and other provisions of Chapter Eleven. Investors may initiate arbitration against the NAFTA Party under the Arbitration Rules of the United Nations Commission on International Trade Law ("UNCITRAL Rules") or the Arbitration (Additional Facility) Rules of the International Center for Settlement of Investment Disputes ("ICSID Additional Facility Rules"). Alternatively, a NAFTA investor may choose to use the registering country's court system.

The Mexican government and courts recognize and enforce arbitral awards. The Embassy has heard of no actions taken in the Mexican courts for an alleged Chapter 11 violation on behalf of U.S. or Canadian firms. There have been numerous cases in which foreign investors, particularly in real estate transactions, have spent years dealing with Mexican courts trying to resolve their disputes. Often real estate disputes occur in popular tourist areas such as the Yucatan Peninsula. American investors should understand that under Mexican law many commercial disputes that would be treated as civil cases in the United States could also be treated as criminal proceedings in Mexico. Based upon the evidence presented, a judge may decide to issue arrest warrants. In such cases Mexican law also provides for a judicial official to issue an "amparo" (injunction) to shield defendants from arrest. U.S. investors involved in commercial disputes should therefore obtain competent Mexican legal counsel, and inform the U.S. Embassy if arrest warrants are issued.

Performance Requirements and Incentives

The 1993 Foreign Investment Law eliminated export requirements (except for maquiladora industries), capital controls, and domestic content percentages, which are prohibited under NAFTA. Foreign investors already in Mexico at the time the law became effective can apply for cancellation of prior commitments. Foreign investors who failed to apply for the revocation of existing performance requirements remained subject to them.

The Mexican federal government has eliminated direct tax incentives, with the exception of accelerated depreciation. A fiscal reform package was passed in September 2007 that includes a Flat Rate Corporate Tax (IETU). This tax limits the deductions that companies are allowed, though changes made at the behest of the business community still allow some credits for previous inventories and investments, as well as for companies that fall under the maquiladora scheme. In 2010, the IETU increased to 17.5%. Investors should follow IETU developments closely.

Most taxes in Mexico are federal; therefore, states have limited opportunity to offer tax incentives. However, Mexican states have begun competing aggressively with each other for investments, and most have development programs for attracting industry. These include reduced price (or even free) real estate, employee training programs, and reductions of the 2% state payroll tax, as well as real estate, land transfer, and deed registration taxes, and even new infrastructure, such as roads. Four northern states -- Nuevo Leon, Coahuila, Chihuahua and Tamaulipas -- have signed an agreement with the state of Texas to facilitate regional economic development and integration. Investors should consult the Finance, Economy, and Environment Secretariats, as well as state development agencies, for more information on fiscal incentives. Tax attorneys and industrial real estate firms can also be good sources of information.

U.S. Consulates have reported that the states in their consular districts have had to modify their incentive packages due to government decentralization. Many states have also developed unique industrial development policies. Sonora, for example, is working to expand the free entry area for tourists (south from the border to the port of Guaymas). Sonora has also implemented long-term agriculture and infrastructure development plans. The government of Yucatan provides information and support to potential investors and business entrepreneurs through several programs that target different industries such as technology, agroindustry and energy exploration. Several states are competing to attract manufacturing in the aerospace industry. The state of Queretaro has made the most advances in the aerospace industry.

A government-owned development bank, Nacional Financiera, S.A., provides loans to companies in priority development areas and industries. It is active in promoting joint Mexican-foreign ventures for the production of capital goods. Nacional Financiera offers preferential, fixed-rated financing for the following types of activities: small and medium enterprises; environmental improvements; studies and consulting assistance; technological development; infrastructure; modernization; and capital contribution. The Mexican Bank for Foreign Trade, Bancomext, offers a variety of export financing and promotion programs. There is an initiative in the Mexican Congress to merge both development banks in order to make them more efficient and streamline the granting of loans.

Mexico's maquiladora and Program for Temporary Imports to produce Exports (PITEX) programs aim to stimulate manufactured exports and operate in largely the same manner. The first focus is on companies that specialize in bond manufacturing and export, while the second is for companies that may have significant domestic sales. In November 2006, the maquiladora and PITEX programs were combined into the renamed IMMEX (Industria Manufacturera, Maquiladora y Servicios de Exportacion) program. The IMMEX program adds services, such as business process outsourcing, to the maquila scheme and also simplifies and streamlines the process under the two previous schemes. The new program continued to exempt companies from import duties and applicable taxes (like Value Added Taxes) on inputs and components incorporated into exported manufactured goods. In addition, capital goods and the machinery used in the production process are tax exempt, but are currently subject to import duties.

Companies interested in investing in industrial activity in Mexico need to follow the new IMMEX guidelines closely, preferably in close consultation with locally based legal advisors. Two export programs implemented during the 1990s, ALTEX (Empresas Altamente Exportadoras) and ECEX (Empresas de Comercio Exterior), also allow expedited VAT returns and financing from government-owned development banks. Please refer to the Ministry of Economy's IMMEX program website at http://www.economia.gob.mx/?P=immex. The Mexican government's recent modifications to the industry's tax regime provide these companies with financial and operational benefits, such as development ofMexico's maquila-servicing and supply industries. Other modifications to the IMMEX Program include: reducing the grounds for which the government can terminate a company's inclusion in the IMMEX Program (and exempts certain qualified companies from being excluded at all); eliminates the requirement that companies submit certain information to both the Secretariat of Economy and the Mexican Tax Service (companies will now only be required to submit the information one time); and extends the temporary importation term for raw materials from 18 months to 36 months for certified companies (or 60 months for companies registered in the Inventory Control System, SECIIT).

In order to maintain competitiveness of maquiladora companies and comply with NAFTA provisions, Mexico has developed "Sectoral Promotion Programs" (PROSEC). Under these programs, most favored nation import duties on listed inputs and components used to produce specific products are eliminated or reduced to a competitive level. These programs comply with NAFTA provisions because import duty reduction is available to all producers, whether the final product is sold domestically or is exported to a NAFTA country. PROSECs supported 24 sectors, including electronic and home appliances, automotive, and auto parts, textile, and apparel, footwear and others. However, since 2008, the government has eliminated some tariffs included in the PROSECs that have not been used for several years or that already have a most favored nation low import duty thanks to a new trade policy implemented by the government. The reduction of PROSECs will conclude in 2012. In December 2008, President Calderon issued in the Official Gazette (Diario Oficial) an immediate and gradual reduction of import duties for more than 10,000 tariffs in order for companies to obtain inputs at competitive prices. When the gradual elimination and reduction of import duties concludes in 2013, the tariff structure will have six basic rates: 0, 5%, 7%, 10%, 15% and 20%. On December 26, 2011 a decree was issued to eliminate 230 tariffs included in 21 of the 24 PROSECs since they already have an equal or higher most favored nation import duty. (http://www.economia.gob.mx/?P=944).

Right to Private Ownership and Establishment

Foreign and domestic private entities are permitted to establish and own business enterprises and engage in all forms of remunerative activity in Mexico, except those mentionedin Section One. Private enterprises are able to freely establish, acquire and dispose of interests in business enterprises. The two most common types of business entities are corporations (Sociedad Anonima) and limited partnerships (Sociedad de Responsibilidad Limitada). Under these legal entities a foreign company may operate an independent company, a branch, affiliate, orsubsidiary company in Mexico. The rules and regulations for starting an enterprise differ for each structure.

For a corporation (Sociedad Anonima):

A) Can be up to 100 percent foreign-owned;
B) Must have a minimum of 50,000 Mexican pesos in capital stock to start;
C) Must have minimum of two shareholders, with no maximum. Board of Directors can run the administration of the company;
D) The enterprise has an indefinite life span;
E) Free transferability of stock ownership is permitted;
F) Operational losses incurred by the Mexican entity or subsidiary may not be used by the U.S. parent company;

G) Limited liability to shareholders.

Limited Liability Company (Sociedad de Responsabilidad Limitada):

A) Can be up to 100 percent foreign-owned;
B) Must have a minimum of 3,000 Mexican pesos in capital stock to start;
C) Must have a minimum of two partners to incorporate a corporation with limited liability. The partners must manage the company but 50 is the maximum number of shareholders;
D) Exists only when the business purpose and partners remain the same;
E) Restricted transferability of partnership shares. Any changes in the partnership composition may cause the partnership to be liquidated;
F) If structured properly, it may offer tax advantages by allowing operational losses incurred by the Mexican entity to be used by the U.S. parent company;
G) Limited liability is afforded the partners.

Protection of Property Rights

Two different laws provide the core legal basis for protection of intellectual property rights (IPR) in Mexico --

the Industrial Property Law (Ley de Propiedad Industrial) and the Federal Copyright Law (Ley Federal del Derecho de Autor). Multiple federal agencies are responsible for various aspects of IPR protection in Mexico. The Office of the Attorney General (Procuraduría General de la Republica, or PGR) has a specialized unit that pursues criminal IPR investigations. The Mexican Institute of Industrial Property (Instituto Mexicano de la Propiedad Industrial, or IMPI) administers Mexico's trademark and patent registries and is responsible for handling administrative cases of IPR infringement. The National Institute of Author Rights (Instituto Nacional del Derecho de Autor) administers Mexico's copyright register and also provides legal advice and mediation services to copyright owners who believe their rights have been infringed. The Mexican Customs Service (Aduanas México) plays a key role in ensuring that illegal goods do not cross Mexico's borders.

Despite strengthened enforcement efforts by Mexico's federal authorities over the past several years, weak penalties and other obstacles to effective IPR protection have failed to deter the rampant piracy and counterfeiting found throughout the country. The U.S. Government continues to work with its Mexican counterparts to improve the business climate for owners of intellectual property.

Mexico is a signatory to at least fifteen international treaties that deal with IPR, including the Paris Convention for the Protection of Industrial Property, the NAFTA, and the WTO Agreement on Trade-related Aspects of Intellectual Property Rights. Though Mexico signed the Patent Cooperation Treaty in Geneva, Switzerland in 1994, which allows for simplified patent registration procedure when applying for patents in more than one country at the same time, it is necessary to register any patent or trademark in Mexico in order to claim an exclusive right to any given product. A prior registration in the United States does not guarantee its exclusivity and proper use in Mexico, but serves merely as support for the authenticity of any claim you might make, should you take legal action in

Mexico. The Anti-Counterfeit Trade Agreement, which sets forth international standards on intellectual property rights enforcement, is currently pending ratification in the Mexican Congress.

Although a firm or individual may apply directly, most foreign firms hire local law firms specializing in intellectual property. The U.S. Embassy's Commercial Section maintains a list of such law firms in Mexico at: http://export.gov/mexico/businessserviceproviders/index.as p

Transparency of Regulatory System

The Federal Commission on Regulatory Improvement (COFEMER), within the Secretariat of Economy, is the agency responsible for reducing the regulatory burden on business. The Mexican government has been making steady progress on this issue in the last few years. On a quarterly basis, these agencies must report to the President on progress achieved toward reducing the regulatory burden. In December 2006, President Calderon replaced the Regulatory Moratorium Agreement, issued by the previous administration, to ensure agencies streamline their regulatory promulgation processes, with the Quality Regulatory Agreement. The new agreement intends to allow the creation of new regulations only when agencies prove that they are needed because of an emergency, the need to comply with international commitments, or obligations established by law.

The federal law on administrative procedures has been a significant investment policy accomplishment. The law requires all regulatory agencies to prepare an impact statement for new regulations, which must include detailed information on the problem being addressed, the proposed solutions, the alternatives considered, and the quantitative and qualitative costs and benefits and any changes in the amount of paperwork businesses would face if a proposed regulation is to be implemented. Despite these measures, many difficulties remain. Foreign firms continue to list bureaucracy, slow government decision-making, lack of transparency, a heavy tax burden, and a rigid labor code among the principal negative factors inhibiting investment in Mexico. The Mexican government, with the OECD, the private sector and several think tanks, is currently working to streamline bureaucracy and procedures, with a particular focus on several Mexican states.

The Secretariat of Public Administration has made considerable strides in improving transparency in government, including government contracting and involvement of the private sector in enhancing transparency and fighting corruption. The Mexican government has established several Internet sites to increase transparency of government processes and establish guidelines for the conduct of government officials. "Normateca" provides information on government regulations; "Compranet" allows for on-line federal government procurement; "Tramitanet" permits electronic processing of transactions within the bureaucracy thereby reducing the chances for bribes; and "Declaranet" allows for online filing of income taxes for federal employees.

Efficient Capital Markets and Portfolio Investment

The Mexican banking sector has strengthened considerably since the 1994 Peso Crisis left it virtually insolvent. Since the crisis, Mexico has introduced reforms to buttress the banking system and to consolidate financial stability. These reforms include creating a more favorable economic and regulatory environment to foster banking sector growth by reforming bankruptcy and lending laws, moving pension fund administration to the private sector, and raising the maximum foreign bank participation allowance. The bankruptcy and lending reforms passed by Congress in 2000 and 2003 effectively made it easier for creditors to collect debts in cases of insolvency by creating Mexico's first effective legal framework for the granting of collateral. Pension reform allows employees to choose their own pension plan. Allowing banks or their holding companies to manage these funds provides additional capital to the banking sector, while the increased competition permits fund managers to focus on investment returns. In December 2007, the Mexican Congress approved amendments to the Law of Credit Institutions (LIC) that included creating a new limited banking license and transferring power from the Mexican tax authority to the Banking and Securities Commission (CNBV), the primary banking regulator.

The financial profile of the banking sector has improved due to the reduction in the problem assets brought about by write-offs, problem loan sales, and the conclusion of most debt-relief programs. These developments, combined with more stringent capital requirements, have contributed to an improvement in the level and composition of capital across the banking system, particularly among the larger institutions.

The banking sector remains highly concentrated, with a handful of large banks controlling a significant market share, and the remainder comprised of regional players and niche banks. The Mexican Tax Authority has approved the opening of several new banks since 2006, including Wal-Mart Bank and Prudential Bank, but the sector's competitive dynamics and credit quality are still being driven by six large banks (Banamex, Bancomer, Santander, HSBC, Banorte and Scotiabank)—five of which are foreign-owned. The newcomers are mostly focused on the unbanked population (D, E market segments) and will present only limited competition to the group of old banks.

Bank lending, especially consumer lending and mortgages, grew rapidly in 2005 and 2006, fueled by lower interest rates and historically low inflation. However, the global financial crisis slowed down all types of lending in 2008 and 2009. According to the CNBV, total loan balances rose to 2.358 trillion pesos ($172 billion dollars) at the end of October 2011, a 13% increase from 2010. Businesses and consumers are demanding more credit as the economy enjoys an export-led rebound, with 2010 posting gross domestic product (GDP) growth of 5.5% and economists widely expecting an expansion of 3.9% at the end of 2010.

The Mexican Banks Association has forecast further double-digit loan growth this year.

Small- and medium-sized businesses still complain of a lack of access to credit, but government-owned development banks have begun to expand their lending to this sector. Despite the expansion, such lending remains low as a percentage of GDP. Private banks argue that due diligence in lending to such business is difficult given the large amount of revenue they keep off the books to avoid increased tax liability. This position may reflect the healthy profits the banks earn from existing business models, currently more than 8% return on assets compared to 2.5% in the United States.

Commercial loans to established companies with well-documented accounts are available in Mexico, but many large companies utilize retained earnings to fund growth. Supplier credit is the main source of financing for many businesses. The largest companies are able to issue debt for their financing needs, tapping into a growing pool of pension funds looking for investment options. Non-bank financing is generally available, however, to large companies with strong credit ratings and important commercial ties with their suppliers -- i.e., companies that could easily procure bank financing.

The Secretariat of Finance and Public Credit sets regulatory policy and oversees the CNBV. Mexico's central bank, the Bank of Mexico (Banxico), also has a regulatory role in addition to setting monetary policy. The Institute for the Protection of Bank Savings (IPAB) handles deposit insurance.

Reforms creating better regulation and supervision of financial intermediaries and fostering greater competition have helped strengthen the financial sector and capital markets. These reforms, coupled with sound macroeconomic fundamentals, have created a positive environment for the financial sector and capital markets, which have responded accordingly. The implementation of

NAFTA opened the Mexican financial services market to U.S. and Canadian firms. Foreign institutions hold more than 70 percent of banking assets and banking institutions from the U.S. and Canada have a strong market presence.. Under NAFTA's national treatment guarantee, U.S. securities firms and investment funds, acting through local subsidiaries, have the right to engage in the full range of activities permitted in Mexico.

Foreign entities may freely invest in government securities. The Foreign Investment Law establishes, as a general rule, that foreign investors may hold 100 percent of the capital stock of any Mexican corporation or partnership, except in those few areas expressly subject to limitations under that law. Regarding restricted activities, foreign investors may also purchase non-voting shares through mutual funds, trusts, offshore funds, and American Depositary Receipts. They also have the right to buy directly limited or non-voting shares as well as free subscription shares, or "B" shares, which carry voting rights. Foreigners may purchase an interest in "A" shares, which are normally reserved for Mexican citizens, through a neutral fund operated by a Mexican Development Bank. Finally, state and local governments, and other entities such as water district authorities, now issue peso-denominated bonds to finance infrastructure projects. These securities are rated by international credit rating agencies. This market is growing rapidly and represents an emerging opportunity for U.S. investors.

Competition from State Owned Enterprises

The Mexican Constitution constrains private investment in the hydrocarbon sector. Articles 27 and 28 specifically establish the monopoly control of the State. Mexico's energy sector faces one of the most restrictive regimes in the world. During the past 15 years, there have been changes in the law to allow some private investment in electric co-generation and self-supply, as well as power generation for export, and, as part of the 2008 energy reform, to permit companies to enter into "performance-linked" contracts for hydrocarbon exploration and drilling. Amendments to the Petroleum Law opened transportation, storage, marketing and distribution of natural gas imports and issued open access regulations for Pemex's natural gas transportation network, as well as retail distribution of Mexico's natural gas and secondary petrochemical industry. Since 2001, the government allowed national and foreign private firms to import liquefied petroleum gas duty-free. There are two main state-owned companies in the energy sector: Petroleos Mexicanos (Pemex), in charge of running the hydrocarbons (oil and gas) sector and the most important fiscal contributor to the country, and the Comision Federal de Electricidad (CFE), in charge of the electricity sector. As required by the Constitution, the electricity sector is also federally owned, with CFE controlling most of installed generating capacity. CFE also holds a monopoly on electricity transmission and distribution. It operates Mexico's national transmission grid, which consists of 27,000 miles of high voltage lines, 28,000 miles of medium voltage lines, and 370,000 miles of low voltage distribution lines. It generates electric power for almost 33.8 million customers (or 100 million people). The infrastructure to generate electric power is made up of 177 generating plants, having an installed capacity of 51,081 megawatts. Reforms to the electricity sector now permit independent power producers to develop projects and sell their electricity to CFE, and for CFE to solicit bids from private companies for new power plant construction: 22.41% of CFE's current installed capacity stems from 21 plants which were built using private capital by Productores Independientes de Energía (PIE). Attempts to reform the sector, including the subsidized rates provided to agricultural users and some consumers, have traditionally faced strong political and social resistance in Mexico, even though the existence of subsidies for residential consumers absorbs substantial fiscal resources.

The President of the United Mexican States appoints the Chief Executive Officer of PEMEX. The Mexican Government closely regulates and supervises the operations of PEMEX through three Ministries: The Secretary of

Energy monitors the company's activities, and serves as the chairman of Pemex's Board of Directors; The Comision Nacional de Hidrocarburos (CNH), which is part of SENER, evaluates Pemex's reserve estimates and provides regulations for Pemex's operations in areas such as deepwater exploration and drilling and gas flaring; the Secretary of Finance and Public Credit incorporates the annual budget and financing program of Pemex and its subsidiaries; and the Secretary of Environment and Natural Resources, in coordination with other federal and state authorities, regulates Pemex's activities that affect the environment.

Pemex has a board of directors, which includes government representatives from the Secretary of Energy, Secretary of Finance, the Secretary of Public Function, and the Office of of the President; four professional members; five representatives from the union; one commissioner; and one independent auditor, which in this case is the private consulting group, KPMG. Pemex's accounting and balance sheets are subject to internal and external audits. The Audit and Performance Evaluation Committee of PEMEX's Board of Directors appoints PEMEX's external auditors. Pemex's financial reports are issued in accordance to Mexico's Generally Accepted Accounting Principles (GAAP), which differ somewhat from U.S. GAAP. PEMEX has registered bond issues in the Securities and Exchange Commission (SEC). Thus, in order to maintain its registration with the SEC, PEMEX has the obligation to file several international standard forms, such as the Form 20-F, on an annual basis. Pemex has also issued bonds in the domestic market, and in accordance with the Stock Market Law, it also has to submit audited quarterly and annual reports to the National Banking and Securities Commission. These reports, along with the annual Hydrocarbons Reserves Report and the Primary and Financial Balance, are published on Pemex's webpage. The state-owned oil company has moved forward in incorporating best corporate and social responsibility practices.

The CFE is a decentralized government agency, duly incorporated, and controls its own assets. Like Pemex, CFE has a Board of Directors, which includes representatives from the Secretariats of Energy, Environment, Social Development, Economy, Finance; Pemex's CEO; and three representatives from the union. CFE's books are also subject to domestic general accounting rules and are reviewed by independent auditors. The Energy and Finance Secretariats approve and submit Pemex's and CFE's budgets to the lower house for approval.

The Servicio Postal Mexicano (Sepomex), or Correos de Mexico, is the national postal service of Mexico and officially retains a monopoly on all mail items under one kilogram. The mail is regulated under Mexico's Communications and Transport Secretariat, and postal service is reserved to the state under Mexico's Constitution. Private delivery under one kilogram is officially illegal, butloopholes in the law have allowed some domestic and foreign privately-owned shippers to provide some delivery services through certified delivery and other advanced-service options to differentiate their business from that of a standard postal delivery. In the past, there were calls for legal reforms that would give Correos de Mexico a strictly enforced monopoly on packages weighing 350 grams or less and require private couriers to charge up to seven times Correos de Mexico's prices, but the government has not moved ahead on this front.

Technically, Correos de Mexico is responsible for financing itself, but the government does subsidize the agency if there is insufficient revenue. Liberalization and privatization of postal markets are not currently on the agenda in Mexico. Correos de Mexico has a Board of Directors presided over by the Ministry of Communications and Transportation. Other members of the Board are: the Secretary of Foreign Affairs, the Secretary of the Economy, the Secretary of Finance, and the Under Secretary of Communications. The Director General is appointed by the President.

Corporate Social Responsibility

Both the private and public sector have taken several actions to promote and develop Corporate Social Responsibility (CSR) in Mexico during the past decade. CSR in Mexico began more as a philanthropic effort, but it has gradually evolved to a more holistic approach, trying to match international standards, such as the OECD Guidelines for Multinational Enterprises and the United Nations Global Compact. Mexico completed in March 2009 the reorganization of their National Contact Point (NCP) as set by OECD's guidelines for MNEs and CSR when the Directorate General for Foreign Investment (DGFI) within the Secretariat of the Economy assumed the office for the implementation and operation of the NCP. The guidelines can be found on the website www.economia.gob.mx. The UN Global Compact reports that there are 209 participants and stakeholders (100 are businesses) from Mexico.

The Mexican Center of Philanthropy (CEMEFI), a well-respected NGO for the promotion of CSR and philanthropy, was created in 1998, and among its achievements has been the creation of the CSR distinctive award in 2001 to those companies that comply with CSR best practices in Mexico and Latin America. To receive the award, CEMEFI takes into consideration whether the company adheres to international standards, including the OCED Guidelines, the UN Global Compact, International Labor Organization, and SA (Social Accountability) 8000, among others. Some of the domestic and foreign companies, of the more than one hundred that have received awards, are: Bimbo, Nestlé, Coca Cola, WalMart, Hewlett Packard, General Electric, Pfizer, and many more.

There is a general awareness of CSR from both producers and consumers for those companies carrying CEMEFI's distinctive logo and there are currently more than two hundred Mexican and foreign companies that have become members of CEMEFI. Following CEMEFI's efforts, the largest and most important business and trade chambers in Mexico created "Aliarse", a high-impact network aimed at promoting CSR in the business sector. In 2005, the Mexican Standards Institute (IMNC) officially issued the CSR standard NMX-SAST-004-IMNC. On November 26, 2010, Mexico officially launched the ISO 26000 Guidance on Social Responsibility, an international standard that offers guidance on socially responsible behavior and possible actions; it does not contain requirements and, therefore, in contrast to ISO management system standards, is not certifiable.

Corporate social responsibility reporting has made progress in the last few years with more companies developing a corporate responsibility performance strategy. The government has also made an effort to implement CSR in state-owned companies such as PEMEX, which has been publishing corporate responsibility reports since 1999. The reports comply with the indicators set forth in the Global Reporting Initiative (GRI) Guidelines and meet the guidelines of the United Nations Global Compact for communication. Perhaps one of the most challenging issues in Mexico is to promote CSR in small and medium-sized enterprises (SMEs). Recently the Secretariat of the Economy has included CSR as a key factor in providing government support to SMEs through various government programs.

Political Violence

Peaceful mass demonstrations are common in the larger metropolitan areas such as Mexico City, Guadalajara, and Monterrey. While political violence is rare, narcotics- and organized-crime-related violence has skyrocketed since 2006. Transnational criminal organizations (TCOs) fighting each other and the government for control of drug-smuggling routes have carried out violent acts unprecedented both in number and nature. 2011 saw more than 12,000 organized crime-related homicides, a six percent increase compared to the previous year, according to widely cited press reports. Cartels use torture and the public dumping of bodies to intimidate their rivals. Institutions, including major media outlets, have been subject to unprecedented attacks, including grenade attacks. As the Mexican government increases the pressure, TCOs continue to expand their operations into any available money-making venture, including kidnappings, extortion, human trafficking, and hijacking cargo shipments, often targeting business owners and others innocent of any involvement in narcotics trafficking.

The United States is working with Mexico more closely than ever to combat organized crime and enhance rule of law through the Merida Initiative. This initiative is a three-year-old program to provide equipment and training to support law enforcement operations and technical assistance for long-term reform and oversight of security agencies, as well as to build a 21st century border and help rebuild communities torn apart by violence. So far the U.S. Congress has appropriated over $1.5 billion USD for this initiative, which has provided, among other things, helicopters and surveillance aircraft, non-intrusive inspection equipment, technical assistance, and training to strengthen investigative techniques, prison systems, border management, and judicial practices. In addition, the Merida Initiative has supported Mexican investments in job creation programs, engaging youth in their communities, expanding social safety nets, and building community confidence in public institutions to create a culture of lawfulness and undercut the allure of the cartels. Though the violence is not political in nature, U.S. Embassy Mexico notes that general security concerns remain an issue for companies looking to invest in the country. Many companies choose to take extra precautions for the protection of their executives. They also report increasing security costs for shipments of goods. The Overseas Security Advisory Council (OSAC) monitors and reports on regional security for American businesses operating overseas. OSAC constituency is available to any American-owned, not-for-profit organization, or any enterprise incorporated in the U.S. (parent company, not subsidiaries

or divisions) doing business overseas
(https://www.osac.gov/).

The Department of State maintains a Travel Warning for
U.S. citizens traveling and living in Mexico, available at:
http://travel.state.gov/travel/cis_pa_tw/tw/tw_5665.html

Corruption

Corruption is pervasive in almost all levels of Mexican
government and society. President Calderon pledged that
his government would fight against corruption in
government agencies at the federal, state and municipal
levels. Aggressive investigations and operations have
exposed corruption at the highest levels of government. In
2008, Calderon launched "Operacion Limpieza,"
investigating and imprisoning alleged corrupt government
officials in enforcement agencies. The Ministry
of Public Administration has the lead on coordinating
government anti-corruption policy. In 2010, the Mexican
Congress considered legislation to prevent the use of
money from organized crime groups in elections. The bill
would sanction, with fines and incarceration, pre-
candidates and candidates that use resources, money, or
vehicles, from illicit sources. The bill is still under review
in the lower chamber of the Congress and has no chance of
passing into law in 2012.

Other government entities, such as the Superior Audit
Office of the Federation (ASF), have been playing a role in
promoting sound financial management and accountable
and transparent government with limited success, as most
Mexican external audit institutions (mostly at the state level)
lack the operational and budgetary independence to protect
their actions from the political interests of the legislators
they serve.

Mexico ratified the OECD Convention on Combating
Bribery in May 1999. The Mexican Congress passed
legislation implementing the convention that same month.
The legislation includes provisions making it a criminal

offense to bribe foreign officials. Mexico is also a party to the OAS Convention against Corruption and has signed and ratified the United Nations Convention against Corruption.

The government has enacted or proposed strict laws attacking corruption and bribery, with average penalties of five to ten years in prison. The Transparency and Access to Public Government Information Act, the country's first freedom of information act, went into effect in June 2003 with the aim of increasing government accountability. Mexico's 31 states have passed similar freedom of information legislation that mirrors the federal law and meets international standards in this field. In 2011, Calderon presented several bills to combat corruption and illicit finance, including the Anti-Corruption Law, which contains sanctions against those who would promote, offer, or give money or any good to a public official, and the Law for the Prevention of Illicit Finance Operations, which created penalties for persons, and their economic agents, who are involved in money laundering or do not report it. The lower chamber of Congress modified the Illicit Finance bill to include NGOs, unions, religious organizations and political parties in the reporting requirement. Currently, the Anti-Corruption Law is pending a second Senate vote, and the Illicit Finance Law is still under consideration in the lower chamber. These bills, when passed into force, will represent a significant step forward in the effort to reduce impunity and stop official corruption. Transparency in public administration at the federal level has noticeably improved, but access to information at the state and local level has been slow.

According to Transparency International's 2011 Index of Corruption Perception, Mexico scored 3 on a scale of 1 to 10 where lower numbers represent a greater perception of corruption. The tally places Mexico in 100th place out of 183 nations, its worst result in 10 years. Nearly one in three Mexicans paid a bribe to speed up paperwork or other administrative processes between June 2009 and June 2010, according to the Global Corruption Barometer by Transparency International. According to this survey, the percentage of people who reported they had paid a bribe increased from 28 percent in 2006 to 31 percent in 2010.

Local civil society organizations focused on fighting corruption are still developing in Mexico. A handful of Mexican non-governmental organizations, including Mexico. Without Corruption and the FUNDAR Center for Analysis and Investigation, work to study issues related to corruption and raise awareness in favor of transparency. The Mexican branch of Transparency International also operates in Mexico. The best source of Mexican government information on anti-corruption initiatives is the Ministry of Public Administration (www.funcionpublica.gob.mx).

Bilateral Investment Agreements

NAFTA governs U.S. and Canadian investment in Mexico. In addition to NAFTA, most of Mexico's eleven other free trade agreements (FTAs) cover investment protection, with a notable exception being the Mexico-European Union FTA. The network of Mexico's FTAs containing investment clauses include Bolivia, Chile, Costa Rica, Colombia, El Salvador, Guatemala, Honduras, Japan, and Nicaragua. A Free Trade Agreement with Peru and also a combined agreement with Central America just passed Mexico's Congress in December 2011.

Mexico has enacted formal bilateral investment protection agreements with 25 countries: 15 European Union countries (Austria, Belgium, Luxembourg, Denmark, Finland, France, Germany, Greece, Italy, Netherlands, Portugal, Spain, Sweden, United Kingdom and the Czech Republic), as well as Australia, Argentina, Cuba, Iceland, India, Panama, South Korea, Switzerland, Trinidad and Tobago, and Uruguay. Bilateral Investment Agreements with China, Belarus and Slovakia were signed in 2009. . Mexico continues to negotiate bilateral investment treaties with Russia, Saudi Arabia, Malaysia, Singapore, Brazil and the Dominican Republic.

The United States and Mexico have a bilateral tax treaty to avoid double taxation and prevent tax evasion. Important provisions of the treaty establish ceilings for Mexican withholding taxes on interest payments and U.S. withholding taxes on dividend payments. The implementation of the flat tax on January 1, 2008 has led to questions as to whether the new tax meets the requirements of the bilateral tax treaty. The U.S. Internal Revenue Service presently allows businesses to credit flat tax against their U.S. taxes and has stated that it will issue a ruling at some future date. Businesses should continue to monitor this issue

Mexico and the United States also have a tax information exchange agreement to assist the two countries in enforcing their tax laws. The Financial Information Exchange Agreement (FIEA) was enacted in 1995, pursuant to the Mutual Legal Assistance Treaty. The agreements cover information that may affect the determination, assessment, and collection of taxes, and investigation and prosecution of tax crimes. The FIEA permits the exchange of information with respect to large-value or suspicious currency transactions to combat illegal activities, particularly money laundering. Mexico is a member of the financial action task force (FATF) of the OECD and has made progress in strengthening its financial system through specific anti-money-laundering legislation enacted in 2000 and 2004. In 2010, Mexico implemented restrictions on U.S. dollar deposits which reduced by 50% the amount of bulk cash repatriated to the United States from the Mexican financial system. However, Mexico needs to approve the proposed Law for the Prevention of Illicit Finance Operations, pending in Congress, to limit peso cash purchases, give the Attorney General's office sole jurisdiction over the investigation and prosecution of money laundering cases, and to oblige more economic agents, such as notaries, consultants, and attorneys to report suspicious operations.

OPIC and Other Investment Insurance Programs

In August of 2004, Mexico and the U.S. Overseas Private Investment Corporation (OPIC) finalized an agreement that enables OPIC to offer all its programs and services in the country. Since then, OPIC has aggressively pursued potential investment projects in Mexico, and the country rapidly became one of the top destinations for projects with OPIC support. OPIC is actively providing over $730 million in financing and political risk insurance support to 17 projects in Mexico. For the third quarter of 2010, OPIC established 4 funds in Mexico in the areas of Housing, Equipment Leasing and two more in Renewable Energy. OPIC also announced its first-ever support of a local currency capital market bond issuance, guaranteeing 2.765 billion pesos of bonds (approximately $217 million) issued in the Mexican market. In addition, OPIC-supported funds are among the largest providers of private equity capital to emerging markets. OPIC's current active projects in Mexico are worth $507.4 million. USD.

The OPIC funds which are currently investing in Mexico include two Alsis Latin America Funds and two Latin Power III funds. For a more detailed description of these funds, including fund contact information and investment strategy, please consult OPIC's website at www.opic.gov.

Labor

Mexico's Federal Labor Law, enacted in 1931 and revised in 1970, is based on article 123 of the Mexican constitution. Under the law, Mexican workers enjoy the rights to associate, collectively bargain, and strike. The law sets a standard six-day workweek with one paid day off. For overtime, workers must be paid twice their normal rate and three times the hourly rate for overtime exceeding nine hours per week. Employees are entitled to most holidays, paid vacation (after one year of service), vacation bonuses, and an annual bonus equivalent to at least two weeks' pay. Companies are also responsible for these additional costs. These costs usually add about 30 to 35 percent to the average employee's salary. Employers must also contribute a tax-deductible two percent of each employee's salary into an individual retirement account. Most employers are required to distribute ten percent of their pre-tax profits for profit sharing. Speaking on behalf of the current administration, the Labor Secretary has repeatedly affirmed that labor reform is and remains one of the top priorities of President Calderon's government. A proposal for the labor reform was introduced by the Calderon administration in March of 2010, but the Congress did not debate it quickly. In November 2010, the primary opposition party, the Institutional Revolution Party (PRI), introduced a different proposal, but both were pulled from Congress' agenda without having been debated before the end of the legislative session. The political strength of the unions remains an issue, and reforms to the labor law – nearly universally acknowledged as necessary – have become highly politicized and complicated by the important elections in 2012. President Calderon is pressing hard to have the labor reforms passed before the end of his administration.

There is a large surplus of labor in the formal economy, largely composed of low-skilled or unskilled workers. On the other hand, there is a shortage of technically skilled workers and engineers. Labor-management relations are uneven, depending upon the unions holding contracts and the industry concerned. Many actors also note that the Mexican government wields veto power in the supposedly neutral and balanced tripartite arrangement of labor-business relations. Mexican manufacturing operations in the textile and garment sectors are experiencing stiff wage competition from Central America and India, but gaining relative wage competition with China in high technology sectors. Mexico's minimum wage averages around US$4.62 per day and is less than a living wage in this OECD country. It is set by the tripartite National Commission for Minimum Wage each year.

The Calderon administration prides itself on reducing the number of strikes in Mexico, but labor unions – especially independent ones like the miners' union, the Mexico City electricians' union, and the National Workers Union (UNT)

– note that absence of strikes is not a reasonable proxy for labor peace. Several long-running issues (notably the miners' union's strike at Cananea and the Mexico City electricians' union's battle to restore their employment) have marred the Mexican government's record. Information on unions registered with federal labor authorities is supposed to be available to the public via Internet (www.stps.gob.mx), but this database is incomplete. Independent unions and international observers also have concerns about so-called "employer protection contracts," or non-representative unions set up to provide the employer with a filler union, thereby protecting the employer from internal grassroots organizing.

Foreign Trade Zones/Free Ports

In addition to the IMMEX programs that operate as quasi-free trade zones, in 2002 Mexico approved the operation of more traditional free trade zones (FTZ). Unlike the previous "bonded" areas that only allowed for warehousing of product for short periods, the new FTZ regime allows for manufacturing, repair, distribution, and sale of merchandise. There is no export requirement for companies operating within the zone to avail themselves of tax benefits. Regulatory guidance for FTZs can be found under Mexico's Customs Law, article 14-D. Most major ports in Mexico have bonded areas ("recinto fiscalizados") or customs agents ("recintos fiscal") within them. Mexico currently has four approved FTZ's, located in San Luis Potosi, Mexico City, Monterrey, and Guanajuato.

Foreign Direct Investment Statistics

Foreign Direct Investment in Mexico (USD Million):

	2007	2008	2009	2010	2011
Total FDI Inflow	31313.4	26888.5	15959	20207.6	19439.8
New Investments	17135.0	11659.5	7494.1	13554.7	8043.1
Earnings Reinvestment	8079.6	7518.7	4250.7	2652.2	7636.7
Inter-company Investment	6098.8	7710.3	4214.1	4000.8	3760.0

Foreign Direct Investment Realized in Mexico by Industrial Sector Destination (USD Million):

	2007	2008	2009	2010	2011
Total FDI Inflow	31313.4	26888.5	15959	20207.6	113808.3
Agriculture	143.5	51.6	35.6	63.5	16.8
Extractive	1685.2	4746.1	830.5	955.4	829.9
Manufacturing	13599.8	7809.3	5659.3	11542.4	8572.0
Electricity & Water	577.6	483.5	59.3	5.1	-218.8
Construction	2316.2	1035.1	702.2	151.1	1239.5
Transportation	296.4	381.3	101.1	159.4	252.9
Financial Services	6516.9	6235.5	2507.1	1833.9	3504.2

Foreign Direct Investment Inflows Realized By Country/Economy of Origin (USD Million)

	2007	2008	2009	2010	2011	Totals
Total FDI	31313.4	26888.5	15959	20207.6	19439.8	113808.3
U.S.A.	12812	11335	7237.5	5519.8	10699.3	47604.5
Spain	5397.8	4882.9	2680.8	1460.7	2911.2	17333.3
France	229.4	198.5	263.6	114.0	161.9	967.2
Virgin Islands	1100.7	1455.6	23.8	11.5	107.9	1699.4
Canada	479.1	3066.1	1621.0	1243.4	668.2	7077.8
Switzerland	605.5	224.3	87.5	243.3	1288.7	2389.3
Germany	642.6	617.0	45.9	306.6	229.9	1842.0
Argentina	21.4	32.7	2.2	-14.2	-1.5	40.6
South Korea	47.5	370.9	75.6	-3.9	-7.5	482.5
Brazil	25.0	93.0	127.8	365.6	299.0	910.4
Taiwan	9.7	33.5	48.3	115.3	25.8	232.6
China	8.6	13.1	32.4	9.1	1.8	65.0
Japan	395.4	142.4	221.4	228.0	664.6	1651.7

Chapter 7: Trade and Project Finishing

How Do I Get Paid (Methods of Payment)

U.S. exporters should be aware that Mexican lending rates are significantly higher than in the U.S., ranging from 25 - 30% per year. Requiring payment either by Confirmed Letter of Credit or Cash In Advance can cost U.S. exporters sales opportunities. While favorable payment terms are important, U.S.companies should consider all financing options available in order to be as competitive as possible.

The economic downturn has put increased pressure on Mexican importers to request longer payment terms as they struggle to finance their operations. In the case of existing contracts, many importers are defaulting on payment deadlines, paying 30 to 45 days late. Exporters are advised to protect themselves from the risk of default by obtaining foreign buyer financing or export insurance from the U.S. ExIm Bank (see below for more information).

It can be difficult to collect from Mexican buyers in cases of non-payment. The U.S. Commercial Service Mexico is currently assisting dozens of U.S. companies in their efforts to obtain payment for products/equipment delivered. It is often necessary to travel to Mexico to meet with the buyer and in many cases to hire a lawyer to handle the case.

U.S. exporters are advised to be cautious and seek counsel when negotiating contracts in Mexico. Once negotiated, be prepared for the unexpected as access to credit in Mexico is limited or costly. Moreover, 90% of the Mexican private sector is comprised of small or medium sized companies, most of which have limited access to credit.

A detailed trade finance guide for U.S. exporters is available at:
http://trade.gov/media/publications/pdf/tfg2008.pdf

A detailed report on financing and payment mechanisms is available at:
http://export.gov/mexico/doingbusinessinmexico/financing u.s.exports/index.asp

How Does the Banking System Operate

Commercial Banks:
Mexico's commercial banks offer a full spectrum of services ranging from deposit accounts, consumer and commercial lending, corporate finance, trusts and mutual funds, to foreign exchange and money market trading.

Currently, 42 banks are operating in Mexico; seven of them have 78% of the market share by total assets and five banks are linked with retail stores.

Mexico's commercial banking sector has been opened to foreign competition. The North American Free Trade Agreement (NAFTA) permits U.S. and Canadian banks or any other foreign bank with a subsidiary in the United States or Canada to establish wholly owned subsidiaries in Mexico. Further, they are allowed to undertake financial inter-mediation and to solicit customers for their parent bank. Almost all major banks, with the exception of Banorte, are under the control of foreign banks.

Following the 1994 peso crisis, banks in Mexico have been very cautious in their lending, preferring to provide loans only to their most sound customers. However, now banks are beginning to implement programs for lending to a wider range of companies, although at relatively high rates. In general, small and medium enterprises (SMEs) have trouble accessing credit.

According to the Bank of Mexico (BANXICO), in the 3 rdquarter of 2011 the main sources of financing were: suppliers 81.9%, commercial banks 34.7%, other companies and/or HQs 22.8%, foreign banks 6.1%, development banks 5.9%, and debt issuance 2.3%. The Mexican Government has enacted several incentives to encourage more lending to SMEs, and banks have followed suit with new lending policies, but it remains to be seen whether the largest segment of the Mexican economy will gain better access to credit.

The Secretariat of Treasury & Public Credit (SHCP), the National Banking and Securities Commission (CNBV), and the Bank of Mexico (BANXICO) are the principal regulators of the banking system.

The Secretariat of Treasury & Public Credit is concerned with institutional issues such as licensing and sets credit and fiscal policies. The National Banking and Securities Commission, a semi-autonomous government agency, is responsible for supervision and vigilance. The Bank of Mexico (the Central Bank) implements these policies and also operates inter-bank check clearing and compensation systems.

The Institute for the Protection of Bank Savings (IPAB, replacing the former institution FOBAPROA) acts as a deposit insurance institution. The Mexican Banking Association (ABM) represents the interests of Mexico's banks.

Development Banks:
The mission of development banks is to fill financing shortfalls in the commercial banking sector. Mexico has seven government-owned development banks that provide services to specific areas of the economy. The dominant institutions are Nacional Financiera (Nafinsa) and the Foreign Trade Bank (Bancomext). These institutions have become primarily second-tier banks that lend through commercial banks and other financial intermediaries such as credit unions, savings and loans, and leasing and factoring companies. Nafinsa's primary program funds micro, small and medium-sized businesses. Nafinsa also undertakes strategic equity investments and contributes equity to joint ventures. Bancomext provides financing to Mexican exports and to small and medium-sized companies. It also offers working capital, project lending, and training to firms in several specific sectors that require support, such as textiles and footwear. The other Mexican development banks are BANOBRAS (National Development Bank for Public Works and Services), FINANCIERA RURAL (Rural Agriculture Bank), BANSEFI (National Savings and Financial Services Bank), BANJERCITO (Mexican Army, Air Force and Navy Bank), and HIPOTECARIA FEDERAL (which finances Mexican homeownership through financial intermediaries)

Non-Banks:
The non-traditional banking sector in Mexico is comprised of exchange houses, credit unions, leasing, factoring companies, financial lending networks with limited objectives (SOFOLES), and financial lending networks with multiple objectives (SOFOMES); SOFOMES are divided in two categories: Regulated Entities (SOFOM ER) and Non Regulated Entities (SOFOM NR).

SOFOLEs must convert to a SOFOM or a traditional lending institution at the latest in 2013. SOFOMEs may offer financial factoring, leasing, loans and/or other credit services but are not allowed to receive deposits from the public.

Foreign-Exchange Controls

There are no controls on the transfer of U.S. dollars into and out of Mexico. This means that profits can be repatriated freely.

However, in an effort to prevent money laundering, the Minister of the Secretariat of Treasury & Public Credit (SHCP) issued a regulation to deposit and exchange pesos into U.S. dollars in Mexican Banks.

The regulation was published in the Official Gazette on June 16, 2010 and was implemented in two stages: a) for individuals from June 21st, 2010 b) for companies within 90 days after the publication of the banking law (September 13, 2010).

Dollar transactions that are processed through on line banking will not change. Nevertheless, according to the new regulation banks must observe the following limits:

•Individuals that are account holders of the bank can deposit no more than
USD$4,000 per month in all banking branches.
•National citizens that are non account holders of the bank can deposit USD $300
dollars daily, but no more than USD $1,500.00 monthly.

•Tourists that are not account holders of the bank can exchange no more than USD $1,500.00 monthly in cash.

It is important to mention that there is no restriction upon the sale of dollars. It is also important to note that when entering or departing Mexico with large amounts of cash the money must be declared and documented.

U.S. Banks and Local Correspondent Banks

There are many U.S.-based banks active in the Mexican market, particularly U.S. brokers and banks working with

ExIm programs. The U.S. Commercial Service Mexico maintains a list of these banks. Please contact Sylvia Montano, Sylvia.Montano@trade.gov for more information

Project Financing

Banks, investor groups, large institutional investors such as insurance companies, public offerings of bonds, and other capital market instruments often provide financing. Such financing is in its infancy in Mexico as the Government of Mexico (GOM) has previously been the owner of these types of projects. The financing required by the GOM has been handled either through large international loan syndication direct to the federal government or its operating entities or through multilateral credits.

Mexico has entered a new era in granting concessions for seaports, airports, railroads, satellite communications, power generation plants, and natural gas distribution systems. In general, Mexican and foreign firms that win bids and tenders need to finance major purchases of both equipment and services.

U.S. Export Import Bank

The Export-Import Bank of the United States (Ex-Im Bank), an independent agency of the federal government, offers various short, medium and long-term export finance and insurance programs. Of specific interest to U.S. exporters are the guarantees for medium-term loans to foreign buyers of capital equipment. Most loans are made by U.S. banks with Ex-Im Bank's guarantee.

Much of Ex-Im Bank's activity is under so-called bundling facilities. A bundling facility is a large medium-term loan made to a Mexican bank by a U.S. bank with the guarantee of Ex-Im Bank. The Mexican bank then makes loans for the purchase of American capital goods to Mexican companies. There also are a number of U.S.-based banks that extend Ex-Im Bank credits in Mexico. The major Mexican commercial banks have signed agreements with Ex-Im Bank to grant lines of credit to Mexican firms that purchase U.S.-made products. Many major Mexican banks (Santander, BBVA-Bancomer, HSBC and others) have Master Guarantee Agreements. Such credits generally are available only to Mexican blue chip companies and to their suppliers with firm contracts.

In February 2010 Ex-Im Bank and the National Development Bank for Public Works and Services (Banobras) of Mexico signed a memorandum of agreement to provide up to $1 billion in financing for Mexico's National Infrastructure Program (NIP) and identify specific projects to be covered by the financing.

Additionally, Ex-Im has made financing for renewable energy a top priority since the inception of its Environmental Exports Programs in 1994 offering competitive financing terms (up to 18 years in some cases) to international buyers for the purchase of U.S. originating environmental goods and services.

The United States is Mexico's biggest trading partner accounting for nearly 50% of the country's imports. As of July 31, 2011 Ex-Im Bank's total exposure in Mexico is $7.4 billion. Mexico remains the largest market in Ex-Im Bank's portfolio and is the ranked first in Latin American/ Caribbean portfolio.

Overseas Private Investment Corporation

Overseas Private Investment Corporation, OPIC, provides medium- to long-term funding through direct loans and loan guaranties to eligible investment projects in developing countries and emerging markets. By complementing the private sector, OPIC can provide financing in countries where conventional financial institutions often are reluctant or unable to lend on such a basis.

OPIC also offers insurance to U.S. investors, contractors, exporters and financial institutions involved in international transactions. Political risk insurance can cover currency inconvertibility, expropriation and political violence, and is available for investments in new ventures, expansions of existing enterprises, privatizations and acquisitions with positive developmental benefits.

Typically, OPIC requires that U.S. investment in a given project represent at least 25% of the total investment value in order to be eligible for assistance. The Overseas Private Investment Corporation (OPIC) offers its full range of programs services in Mexico, as of September 2010 (the most recent statistics available), Mexico is OPIC's largest country with exposure at approximately USD $1 billion.

U.S. Trade and Development Agency

The U.S. Trade and Development Agency (USTDA) provides funding for feasibility studies and other forms of technical assistance to help promote U.S. exports. By assisting U.S. firms to become involved in the early stages of project development, USTDA leverages U.S. exports during the implementation stages. USTDA works closely with the various development banks, including the World Bank and the Inter-American Development Bank, to help U.S. firms take advantage of those banks' projects. Additionally, in the case of a competitive bid for a large infrastructure project, USTDA can offer a de minimus training grant, or another form of technical assistance, to help the U.S. Company or consortium make their bid more attractive. USTDA has an active program in Mexico, funding projects in a wide range of sectors.

In 2009, USTDA provided over $2 million in support of priority infrastructure projects that further the objectives of the Mexico's National Infrastructure Program, including feasibility studies for the modernization of three airports. During 2010, USTDA funded two reverse trade missions in health care information technology, multimodal transportation and sponsored a project identification mission for the Mexican renewable energy sector. In 2011, USTDA supported feasibility studies in the renewable energy industry.

U.S. Small Business Administration

The U.S. Small Business Administration (SBA) provides financial and business development assistance to encourage and help small businesses in developing export markets. The SBA assists businesses in obtaining the capital needed to explore, establish, or expand international markets. SBA's export loans are available under SBA's guaranty program. Prospective applicants should tell their lenders to seek SBA participation, if the lender is unable or unwilling to make the loan directly.

SBA also offers an Export Revolving Line of Credit (ERLC) program that is designed to help small businesses obtain short-term financing to sell their products and services abroad. The program guarantees repayment to a lender in the event an exporter defaults. The ERLC protects only the lender from default by the exporter; it does not cover the exporter should a foreign buyer default on payment. Lenders and exporters must determine whether foreign receivables need credit risk protection.

Inter-American Development Bank

The Inter-American Development Bank (IADB) finances public sector projects in Mexico and the other 25 borrowing countries in Latin America and the Caribbean. In 2011 the approved loans in Mexico for the public sector (Sovereign Guaranteed Operations-SGO) were 1.5 billion USD and for the private sector (Non Sovereign Guaranteed Operations- NSGO) 9.7 billion USD. The IADB has focused its lending programs on infrastructure needs in Mexico, while the World Bank has favored human resource development and structural reform initiatives.

U.S. companies are eligible to compete for contract awards from public sector executing agencies. However, in contrast to trade finance institutions, U.S. companies do not apply directly to the IADB. U.S. companies interested in competing for public sector projects financed by the IADB may maximize their chances of winning by contracting a local partner in Mexico. The U.S. Commercial Service maintains an office in the IADB to assist U.S. companies in taking advantage of IADB funded projects.

World Bank

The World Bank is a multi-lateral development bank that provides loans to developing countries with the stated goal of reducing poverty. World Bank is comprised of two institutions: the International Bank for Reconstruction and Development (IBRD) and the International Development Association (IDA). IBRD is active in Mexico, supporting large-scale infrastructure projects such as highways, airports, and power plants.

Mexico has the second largest World Bank portfolio in Latin America. During FY11 the World Bank approved projects for a total of $2.7 billion USD in key sectors such as health, education and sustainable and environment.

The International Finance Corporation (IFC), the private sector arm of the World Bank, promotes infrastructure development, particularly water and renewable energy as well as inclusive markets such as microfinance, housing, health and education.

Particularly given the tight credit market, it is common for governments to leverage financing from several sources, (The World Bank, Export Credit Agencies, private equity funds, etc.) when developing large projects.

Chapter 8: Business Travel

Business Customs

Mexican businesspeople in major cities give a great deal of importance to appearances and therefore we advise wearing professional attire when meeting with prospective business partners in Mexico.

Participation in business lunches is very important to succeed in Mexico. Before beginning a business discussion, it is common to discuss family, recent events or other social themes. Mexicans are accustomed to smoking and drinking freely at business meals. Business lunches can span two hours or more.

Patience is key to doing business in Mexico. Business meetings in Mexico will often take longer than they would in the United States. Etiquette often includes small talk before business.

Mexican social etiquette makes it difficult to say no. Therefore, yes does not always mean yes. In conversation,

Mexicans emphasize tactful and indirect phrasing, and may be more effusive than Americans with praise and emotional expressions. Do not be overly aggressive while negotiating. It is considered rude.

The concept of time is flexible in Mexico. Guests to social events (except in the case of cities in the North) can arrive up to an hour late. However, punctuality is observed for most business and government appointments.

Business cards are used extensively. Come with a large supply.

Travel Advisory

For detailed information about travel advisory information from the State Department, please click on: http://travel.state.gov/travel/cis_pa_tw/tw/tw_5665.html

Visa Requirements

All U.S. citizens must have a passport or passport card to enter Mexico.

There is a single visa form for tourist and business visitors, valid for 30 days upon entry with no fee. This form is normally distributed on all arriving aircraft. Business visitors must be careful not to enter as a tourist if their reason for visiting includes any of the following activities:

- •Business meetings
- •Trade events
- •Consulting
- •Technical support
- •Marketing

Contracts and other business agreements entered into while an American visitor to Mexico is traveling on tourist rather than business status are not legal. There have been rare instances of immigration authorities detaining visitors doing business while on tourist status, resulting in fines up to USD$2,000. Immigration officials also have the authority to bar such travelers from obtaining visas in the future.

Immigration status can be adjusted fairly easily while in country for tourists who later find they want to do business. In Mexico City, visa status can be converted at the following immigration office, located not far from several major business hotels:

Delegación Regional
Instituto Nacional de Migracion (INM)
Lic. Mario Velazquez Santiago
Avenida Ejercito Nacional No. 862
Col. Los Morales, Polanco
11570 Mexico, D.F.
Phone: 2581-0100 x 32005

If a U.S. businessperson wants to reside in Mexico and work on a more permanent basis, it is necessary to obtain an FM-3 immigration form. This form may be obtained with validity up to one year, renewable up to a total of five years. The cost is about USD$165 at the current exchange rate.

To obtain the FM-3 the traveler must present any of the following documents:

- Valid passport, or
- Proof that the traveler is engaged in international business and that he will receive his income from the U.S. company
(e.g. a letter from the U.S. employer). A verbal declaration may be acceptable.

IMPORTANT NOTE: All foreign visitors should keep their Visitor Card (FMM) bearing the official "FEE PAID" stamp as it must be surrendered upon departure from the country. It is extremely important to keep this form in a safe location. Upon exiting the country at a Mexican Immigration (INM) departure check point, U.S. citizens are required to turn in this form. We are aware of cases where U.S. citizens without their FMM have been required to change their flight (at personal expense), file a police report with local authorities regarding the missing document, and visit an INM office to pay a fine and obtain a valid exit visa. In other cases, travelers have been able to continue their journey after paying a fine.

If you enter Mexico by land and expect to depart by air, be sure to request the FMM when entering Mexico. It is not automatically given and if you then return to the United States by air you are subject to a fine.

For further information please visit the Mexican Ministry of Tourism web site at: http://www.sectur.gob.mx/
.

U.S. Companies that require travel of foreign businesspersons to the United States should allow for sufficient time for visa issuance if required. Visa applicants should go to the following links.

State Department Visa Website:
http://travel.state.gov/visa/visa_1750.html

U.S. Embassy Mexico Visa Information:
http://mexico.usembassy.gov/visas.html

Telecommunications

Telephone Services:
Telephone service is usually reliable and most parts of Mexico have direct dialing to the United States. Telephone service is heavily taxed in Mexico, and fees are relatively high. MCI, and AT&T calling cards may be used in Mexico. Cellular telephones are available and widely used.

While traveling throughout Mexico, the two main mobile carriers, Telcel and Movistar have national coverage and international roaming services. Best reception is found on federal highways and the top 50 cities in the country, including beach resorts. Nevertheless, the CDMA operator Iusacell has countrywide coverage and roaming agreements in the U.S. with Sprint and Verizon. If you bring your mobile phone, chances are that you will be able to use it while traveling to Mexico, regardless of the company and technology (GSM, CDMA or PTT) you use.

For mobile office device users (Blackberry, Palm, etc.) roaming services not only apply for voice services, but also for data services. This means you can also receive email on your mobile phone if you have contracted such a service in the U.S. However, if you do not have an international plan, (voice and data) roaming fees can be substantial.

Local Mobile Operators are:
Telcel (GSM / TDMA):
http://www.telcel.com

MóviStar (GSM / CDMA):
http://www.telefonicamovistar.com.mx

Iusacell (CDMA / 3G):
http://www.iusacell.com.mx

Nextel – Trunking Services:
http://www.nextel.com.mx

Comisión Federal de Telecomunicaciones:
http://www.cofetel.gob.mx

Internet Services:
Tourist and business hotels provide Internet services, sometimes wirelessly, in rooms, or at a minimum, in business centers. Internet hotspots are now becoming more common. Because Internet penetration in residential areas is relativelylow, Mexico has a proliferation of Internet cafés that offer Internet access.

Transportation

Mexico City, Guadalajara, Monterrey, Tijuana, Queretaro, and other Mexican cities have frequent direct and non-stop flights from major U.S. cities. American carriers to Mexico include: American, Delta, U.S. Airways, and United. Mexican carriers providing scheduled service within Mexico include Aeromexico, Volaris, and Interjet.

The Mexico City Benito Juarez International Airport offers a fixed price (depending on destination) taxi service to any point in the city. Tickets are purchased at a booth just outside the baggage claim area. This taxi service is regulated and monitored by the government. A similar service is available at other airports around the country. For security reasons, it is recommended that travelers do not use any other private taxi services offered on-site. It is important to ONLY use registered "sitio" taxi services throughout the country. Please see safe taxi recommendations under the "Threats to Safety and Security" section at: http://travel.state.gov/travel/cis_pa_tw/cis/cis_970.html#safety

Language

Spanish is the official language of Mexico. While many people in the large cities speak some English, it may be difficult for them to conduct detailed discussions. Non-Spanish- speaking visitors to Mexico may wish to hirean interpreter. It is considered courteous for U.S. business people to speak a few words of Spanish. Many mid and high-level government officials and business executives speak English, and many are U.S.-educated.

Health

A high standard of medical care is available in the principal cities from private hospitals and doctors. Many private Mexican doctors have U.S. training and speak English.

In Mexico City, U.S. Embassy staff requiring urgent medical care generally visit the ABC Hospital (tel: 5230-8000; emergency ward 5230-8161). Other good private hospitals and clinics located around the city include the

Angeles Group (various locations); Medica Sur (south Mexico City), and Clinica Londres (central). In Monterrey, the Consulate recommends the following hospitals: Christus Muguerza, CIMA Santa Engracia , and San Jose. All are well-equipped and offer good quality care comparable to hospitals in the United States. In Guadalajara, U.S. Consulate staff requiring urgent medical care can select from the following options: Hospital Puerta de Hierro (tel: (33) 3848-2100), Hospital Angeles del Carmen (tel: (33) 3813-1224), and Hospital San Javier (tel: (33) 3669-0222) .

Visitors should follow standard international dietary precautions in Mexico. It is best to drink bottled beverages without ice. Bottled water is readily available. Raw salads should not be consumed, all fruits should be peeled, only pasteurized dairy products should be consumed, and meat should be ordered well done. Hotels and business restaurants in general cater to foreign visitors and fulfill all sanitary requirements. Many American fast food chains have franchises in Mexico with similar standards as in the United States.

Air pollution in the Valley of Mexico (Mexico City and adjacent areas) is chronic. Contaminants in excess of U.S. and Mexican standards pollute the air many days during the year. Air pollution is at its peak from November to April, during the dry season, and may aggravate allergy and cardiopulmonary problems. The relatively high altitude of Mexico City, a long winter dry season, and air pollution can cause irritation of the respiratory tract, nose, and eyes - the latter especially for those who use contact lens.

Visitors to Mexico City should remember the high altitude and be prepared to move slowly and get sufficient rest, until they have adjusted. Upon arrival in Mexico City, increased respiration, rapid heart rate, and mild dizziness may occur while visitors acclimate to the higher altitude. Insomnia, fatigue, circulatory problems, symptoms of dehydration, and nausea are common, but pass quickly. Alcoholic beverages have a stronger effect. Newcomers may find it beneficial to drink plenty of water.

Local Time, Business Hours, and Holidays

Mexico spans several time zones, as does the United States. From the Yucatán Peninsula to Tijuana, there is a three-hour time difference. Mexico City and Central Mexico is Central Standard Time (CST).

On holidays, banks will not open and most businesses will be closed. Be aware of the popular "puentes". When holidays fall near the weekend, they are rapidly converted into long weekends and are not a good time to schedule business trips.

Temporary Entry of Materials and Personal Belongings

Temporary imports for manufacturing, transformation, and repair under the Maquila and Pitex programs are subject to payment of duties, taxes and compensatory fees. Other temporary imports from the U.S., however, do not pay import duties, taxes or fees, but they must comply with all other obligations set forth in Article 104 of the Mexican Customs Law. Please see Chapter 5, Temporary Entry, for more details.

Mexico began accepting ATA Carnets on May 16, 2011 for the temporary import of commercial samples, professional equipment and booths and other materials for exhibitions and fairs. Goods can stay in Mexico for up to six months without having to pay any import duties or taxes. Carnets will need to be registered before entering Mexico. Mexican customs has authorized the following ports of entry to process carnets: Tijuana, Juarez, Nuevo Laredo, Altamira, Veracruz, Manzanillo, Monterrey, Guadalajara, Cancun, Mexico City Airport, Cabo San Lucas and Santa Rosalia. Carnet users and freight forwarders planning to use carnets to Mexico are strongly advised to contact a Carnet Specialist well in advance to discuss their needs and the requirements of Mexican customs. More information about the program can be found at:

http://www.atacarnet.com/advisory/mexico-carnet-detailsor
by emailing Info@ATACarnet.com

.

Chapter 9: Contacts, Market Research, and Trade Events

Contacts

Mrs. Ann Bacher
Minister Counselor for Commercial Affairs
United States Trade Center
Liverpool # 31
Col. Juárez
06600 México, D.F.
Phone: (011-52-55) 5140-2601
Fax: (011-52-55) 5705-0065
Mail: P.O. Box 9000
Brownsville, TX 78520-0900
E-mail: ann.bacher@trade.gov
http://export.gov/mexico/

Mr. Adam Shub
Minister Counselor for Economic and Environmental
Affairs
Embassy of the United States of America
Paseo de la Reforma # 305, Piso 4
Col. Juárez
06500 México, D.F.
Phone: (011-52-55) 5080-2810

Fax: (011-52-55) 5080-2394
Mail: P.O. Box 9000
Brownsville, TX 78520-0900
Email: shubam@state.gov
http://www.usembassy-mexico.gov

Mr. Dan Berman
Minister Counselor for Agricultural Affairs
Embassy of the United States of America
Paseo de la Reforma # 305, Piso 2
Col. Juárez
06500 México, D.F.
Phone: (011-52-55) 5080-2847
Fax: (011-52-55) 5080-2776
Mail: P.O. Box 9000
Brownsville, TX 78520-9000
Email: agmexico@usda.gov
http://www.usembassy-mexico.gov

Mr. Garth Thorburn
Director, U.S. Agricultural Trade Office
United States Trade Center
Liverpool # 31
Col. Juárez
06600 México, D.F.
Phone: (011-52-55) 5140-2611
Fax: (011-52-55) 5535-8357
Mail: P.O. Box 9000
Brownsville, TX 78520-0900
Email: atomexico@usda.gov
http://www.mexico-usda.com/

U.S. Agricultural Trade Office, Monterrey
Blvd. Diaz Ordáz # 140 Torre 2, Floor 7
Col. Santa María
64650 Monterrey, Nuevo León
Phone: (011-52-81) 8333-5289
Fax: (011-52-81) 8333-1248
Mail: P.O. Box 9002
Brownsville, TX 78520-9002
E-mail: atomonterrey@usda.gov

http://www.mexico-usda.com/

Mr. John Howell
Principal Commercial Officer
U.S. Consulate General, Monterrey
Av. Constitución # 411 Pte.
64000 Monterrey, Nuevo León
Phone: (011-52-81) 8047-3223 / 8047-3100
Fax: (011-52-81) 8047-3188 / 8047-3355
Mail: P.O. Box 9002
Brownsville, TX 78520-9002
E-mail: John.Howell@trade.gov
http://export.gov/mexico/

Mr. Paul Kullman
Principal Commercial Officer
U.S. Consulate General, Guadalajara
World Trade Center
Av. Mariano Otero # 1249 Torre Pacífico, Piso 4
44530 Guadalajara, Jalisco
Phone: (011-52-33) 3615-1140
Fax: (011-52-33) 3615-7665
Mail: P.O. Box 9001
Brownsville, TX 78520-0901
E-mail: paul.kullman@trade.gov
http://export.gov/mexico/

Government of Mexico:
Secretaría de Economía (SE)
(Former SECOFI-Secretariat of Commerce and Industrial
Development):
http://www.economia.gob.mx

Instituto Mexicano de la Propiedad Industrial (IMPI)
(Mexican Institute of Industrial Property and Technological
Development):
http://www.impi.gob.mx

Secretaría de Educación Pública (SEP)
(Secretariat of Public Education):

http://www.sep.gob.mx

Secretaría de Energía (SENER)
(Secretariat of Energy):
http://www.energia.gob.mx

Secretaría de Medio Ambiente, Recursos Naturales
(SEMARNAT)
(Secretariat of the Environment, Natural Resources):
http://www.semarnat.gob.mx

Secretaría de Comunicaciones y Transportes (SCT)
(Secretariat of Communications and Transport):
http://www.sct.gob.mx

Chambers of Commerce:
American Chamber of Commerce in Mexico, A.C.:
http://www.amcham.com.mx

U.S.- Mexico Chamber of Commerce:
http://www.usmcoc.org

Cámara de Comercio Hispana de los Estados Unidos
United States Hispanic Chamber of Commerce:
http://www.ushcc.com

Cámara Nacional de Comercio de la Ciudad de México
(CANACO)
(National Chamber of Commerce of Mexico City):
http://www.ccmexico.com.mx

Confederación de Cámaras Nacionales de Comercio,
Servicios y Turismo
(Confederation of National Chambers of Commerce):
http://www.concanacored.com

Cámara Nacional de la Industria de la Transformación
(National Manufacturing Industry Chamber):
http://www.canacintra.org.mx

Confederación de Cámaras Industriales de los Estados
Unidos Mexicanos
(Confederation of Industrial Chambers of Mexico):
http://www.concamin.org.mx

Asociación Nacional de Importadores y Exportadores de la
República Mexicana, A.C.
Association of Importers and Exporters of Mexico:
http://www.anierm.org.mx

It should be noted that there are hundreds of specialized
and regional associations and
chambers in Mexico, which could not be included here.

Market Research

To view market research reports produced by the U.S.
Commercial Service please go to the following website:
http://export.gov/mrktresearch/index.asp

Please note that these reports are only available to U.S.
citizens and U.S. companies. Registration to the site is
required, but free of charge.

Trade Events

Please click on the link below for information on upcoming
trade events.
http://export.gov/tradeevents/index.asp

For a listing of trade events in Mexico:
http://export.gov/mexico/tradeevents/eventsinmexico/eg_m
x_031541.asp

Chapter 10: Guide to Our Services

The U.S. Commercial Service offers customized solutions to help your business enter and succeed in markets worldwide. Our global network of trade specialists will work one-on-one with you through every step of the exporting process, helping you to:

- Target the best markets with our world-class research
- Promote your products and services to qualified buyers
- Meet the best distributors and agents for your products and services
- Overcome potential challenges or trade barriers

For more information on the services the U.S. Commercial Service offers U.S. businesses, please go to:

http://www.buyusa.gov/mexico/en/business_opportunities_mexico.html

http://mexico.usembassy.gov/

The Internationalist

www.internationalist.com